AMP UP YOUR *Life*

How to Thrive with Your
<u>A</u>ttitude
<u>M</u>indset and
<u>P</u>erspective

DEANNE KAUFFMAN

AMP Up Your Life: How to Thrive With Your Attitude, Mindset, and Perspective Copyright 2022 Deanne Kauffman.

All rights reserved. No part of this publication may be reproduced, distributed, or transmitted in any form or by any means, including photocopying, recording, or other electronic or mechanical methods, without the prior written permission of the publisher, except in the case of brief quotations embodied in critical reviews and certain other noncommercial uses permitted by copyright law.

Although the author and publisher have made every effort to ensure that the information in this book was correct at press time, the author and publisher do not assume and hereby disclaim any liability to any party for any loss, damage, or disruption caused by errors or omissions, whether such errors or omissions result from negligence, accident, or any other cause.

Adherence to all applicable laws and regulations, including international, federal, state, and local governing professional licensing, business practices, advertising, and all other aspects of doing business in the US, Canada, or any other jurisdiction, is the sole responsibility of the reader and consumer.

Neither the author nor the publisher assumes any responsibility or liability whatsoever on behalf of the consumer or reader of this material. Any perceived slight of any individual or organization is purely unintentional.

The resources in this book are provided for informational purposes only and should not be used to replace the specialized training and professional judgment of a health care or mental health care professional.

Neither the author nor the publisher can be held responsible for the use of the information provided within this book. Please always consult a trained professional before making any decision regarding treatment of yourself or others. For more information, email deannekauffman4@gmail.com

ISBN: 979-8-88759-434-7

I have made a diligent effort to locate the author and copyright ownership of all material I quote in this book; however, because I have collected so many clippings for over thirty years, I often have no way of identifying the original source. If readers of this book know the correct source of items not designated, I would appreciate hearing from you so proper corrections can be made, and credit is given.

Some names have been changed to protect their identities. Also, my memories are imperfect but I'm sharing my journey to the best of my knowledge and remembrance. My sharing is not intended to hurt anyone, but to only help others learn that the truth can set them free from what is holding them back and to succeed in life.

What a blessing to see the gifts unfold in Deanne's writing. From beginning to end, she shares her life with honesty and love to help others with struggles in their darkest hours. Each word shares her heart and is a joy to read and use practically in our lives. —Lori

"Great hope and inspiration." —Amy, Illinois.

"I love her idea about writing down how I would like to feel." —Nancy, Michigan.

"Deanne is an enthusiastic vessel incredibly anointed in telling her scars turned into hope for the world." —Joy, Florida.

"She touched my soul." —Wendy.

"Deanne's trials and her methods for overcoming them strike a chord with many," —Ginny, Bonita Springs.

Contents

Contents 5

Dedication 7

Acknowledgments 9

Preface 11

Introduction 15

Chapter 1: What Do You Want? 21

Chapter 2: A.M.P. up Your Thought Life 49

Chapter 3: Enjoy Life: 65

Chapter 4: Lighten Up and Laugh 65

Chapter 5: Fifteen Years of Trials 83

Chapter 6: A Fairy Tale New Start 117

Chapter 7: If You Really Want to Thrive 127

Chapter 8: Write Your Story 143

Chapter 9: "Do You Hear What I Hear?" 153

Chapter 10: Broken: When You Have No Hope 157

Chapter 11: You Got This 177

Dedication

This book is dedicated to my mother, who has endured much more pain and trials than I can imagine. She is a lady who is an example of keeping her faith through it all. A woman that taught me to read to get the help I needed. She is the strongest woman I know.

Thank you, Mom, for always loving, supporting, and encouraging me.

Your daughter, DeeDee

Acknowledgments

My appreciation and thanks go to my family for allowing me many working hours without pay, believing it would be worth it in the end. Special appreciation goes to Judi for asking me to speak for the first time, leading me to change my life completely. I'm so thankful, and in awe of the man I get to call my husband Duane, best friend, partner, and lover, who supports me and my ambitions for speaking, writing, and singing.

Special thanks and acknowledgment also to the following individuals, groups, and companies:

My Writer's Group

Shannon Ethridge's Blast Program

Self-Publishing School

Carol Kent's Speak-Up Conference

PREFACE

My mother started teaching me about attitude at a young age. She always had quotes or poems on the fridge about it. Little did she or I know how much those sayings would influence me, that it would start a pattern of searching for the positive or how badly I would need it later in life. She loved to read. I remember her sitting all day long reading. I love and long to do the same, though I cannot read as much as I would like. As I write, I have four children in the house who love to interrupt me every few minutes.

I'm an avid self-help, nonfiction book reader. Authors and psychologists have helped me learn how to live life. I believe I can help someone as well. We all have knowledge within us that we can help each other with. I have overcome fifteen long years of trials that I thought would never end, and I have learned to Thrive through whatever comes my way. What are you walking through right now? Are you stuck in past heartaches, mistakes, and disappointments? Have you suffered deep trauma?

As a little girl, I remember standing at our stereo system wearing giant headphones, singing my heart out to Barbara Streisand. A friend of ours came to the door unknowingly to me. He was an outstanding singer. My dad used to sing in quartets. I turned around to see this young gentleman and my parents laughing at my singing. I was devastated. From then on, I didn't let anyone hear me sing. I would go for walks and sing in our field or the woods. I *loved* to sing. But I took that moment and let it close off my singing in front of anyone.

I went through so many trials for so long that it seemed all I knew was pain. But as Victor Frankl says in his book about surviving the concentration camps, *Man's Search for Meaning*:

> ***After all, he has suffered, there's nothing he need fear anymore---except his God.***

I'm strong because of all I have been through. There isn't much I'm afraid of. I've studied, learned, and gained enlightenment and am excited to share it with you. I'm a person like you trying to figure out life. If you're going through a challenging trial, I want you to know I'm so sorry. There's no magic answer or solution to alleviate your pain. But please don't ever give up hope for a better tomorrow. That thought, in itself, brings healing.

My mom once drew a picture of a heart ripped into pieces but sewn back together with strands of love. One day on my way to work, I saw a desk with roadside trash. It was a solid wood desk covered in layers of paint. I sanded it, cut down the legs, and repainted it to make a beautiful coffee table. I love to take something old, worn out, unwanted or broken, and make it new.

I've always said paint covers a multitude of sins. It refreshes and beautifies what once was dirty, stained, or ugly. Even old, out-of-date, and obsolete things can have great value. I'm a realist. I accept reality the way it is but make the most of it. I focus on what's good, not the bad. Unlike psychotherapy, a personal coach doesn't mull over fixing things in the past but only looks toward the future. At a speaker's conference, Tammy Whitehurst declared, "If you're not dead, you're not done." ***You're*** not done, my friend. There's *more* to your life than pain and suffering. There's more to life than rewards and accolades. You're here for a reason. Someone needs the gifts, talents, and wisdom inside you. You can Thrive!

I'm just a girl who has been through the wringer and can finally say I've come out a winner. I can't wait to share with you what has helped me Thrive. I have learned to let go of all that was holding me back. I hope to inspire and encourage you to keep fighting, be an overcomer, and thrive as well. I want you to say, "I believe I can Thrive through whatever comes my way." After so many years, I can look back and realize how ***strong*** I am because of all I've been through. You can be strong too. There's hope no matter what the circumstances.

Introduction

Many different things have "changed my life," a good self-help book, famous quotes, a mantra, or a Bible verse. One particular saying was, "Give up the good to go for the Great." That can be hard to do. Letting go of good things is hard. What about letting go of the bad? Why is that hard, too, sometimes? Like the bad things that happen to us. We can mull them around in our brains forever. They can keep us stuck.

For the past few years, I've kept a small chalkboard hanging at my desk that I change the saying on when one speaks to me in a unique way. These sayings or mantras help remind me what to focus on. I look at it when I doubt what I'm doing is right, and it gives me the confidence to keep going. Today it says:

"Finish what you started last year. You've got what it takes. Show them what you're made of."

I want this book to help you find what inspires *you* to keep going. It would be best if you found something to grab hold of, give you strength and determination, and keep your focus and hope.

Dream:

We'll begin this journey with what your biggest dreams are. Do you know what you want? Have you ever sat down and listed your biggest dreams and goals? I spent most of my life letting my day dictate what happened to me. I didn't realize I could choose what happens, and so can you.

Thoughts:

Next, we'll talk about mindset. I listened to a TED talk with Dr. Alia Crum. She talked about our mindset and how our thoughts have a sizable impact on the results we get.

I've learned from experience that my thoughts do have a significant impact on my results. Our attitude is everything. Wherever our focus goes is what comes to fruition. Where's your focus most of the time?

When we keep replaying troubling thoughts, it perpetuates those worrisome thoughts.

Kind of like a snowball rolling down a hill,
> as more snow sticks to it,
>> the heavier it gets,
> the more it weighs,
and snow keeps sticking,
> until you can't push it anymore because it's so LARGE.

Dave Ramsey would say compound interest. If you keep investing for the long term, the faster and greater it grows.

It's the same with our thoughts. They can negatively attack us. A loved one may communicate something, and we take it the wrong way, or we assume they meant something they didn't, and we replay our assumptions over and over. Then, we react negatively to them based on speculation.

So, our thoughts significantly impact what happens to us and how we feel. Learning to quickly stop a negative thought and exchange it for a good one is a skill worth working on. I'll have more *"thoughts"* on this later.

Enjoy Life:

In Chapter Three, we dig into laughter. We should:
L O
  L

Would you say that you get up every day to enjoy life and spend time laughing? Fun is my biggest challenge. And I have a feeling it is for most of us. We need to lighten up more often because laughter is the best medicine. Do you know what kind of tea is hard to swallow? (I'm a big tea drinker.) Reality! Laughter helps us face reality. It's the honey in the tea. I also call myself a realist; I know I need to lighten up and laugh more often. How about you?

Thrive:

Bethany Hamilton is one example of thriving when life hits you hard. At thirteen years old, Hamilton had her left arm bitten off by a shark during a surfing accident. Instead of succumbing to the tragedy, she returned to her surfboard one month later and relearned how to surf with only one arm. Two years later, Bethany won first place in the Explorer Women's Division of the NSSA (National Scholastic Surfing Association) Championships.

Barbara Johnson wrote a book, *Stick a Geranium in Your Hat and Be Happy*. Her husband was in a near-fatal accident and slowly recovered from severe, debilitating injuries. She lost one son in Vietnam, another son to a drunk driver, and the third son to a homosexual lifestyle and eleven years of separation. But despite her difficulties, she learned that pain is inevitable to us all, and we can choose to pick flowers instead of weeds. She went on to write many books and was a speaker. Her example showed me that if she could go through similar things that I had experienced and accomplish so much, then I could too.

Story

What's your life story? We're all shaped by our family, heredity, and experiences. I think it's so important to share our stories with each other. Doing so can create a fresh appreciation for our own lives. We're so intrinsically different, and I don't think we realize how important it is to share our uniqueness with the world.

My husband is a naturally gifted musician. He picks up any instrument and plays it without notes or formal teaching. He doesn't realize the incredible gift that is.

I want you to discover what *your* gift is. You're here for a reason, and you have something special no one else has that needs to be shared. Finding our gifts helps us climb up out of whatever pit or trial we may be struggling in. We need faith that we can Thrive no matter what comes our way. I believe you can overcome any past or current abuse, regret, loss, diagnosis, mistake, disappointment, or trauma and Thrive through it all.

Broken

I must talk about depression. We might break down for a moment, a day, or get stuck for months. If you want to fix something that's broken, you have to find all the pieces and carefully, in the correct order, put them back together. Taking care of yourself and your particular needs is this chapter's focus.

Instinct

I can't wait to delve into our inner voice and instinct. Do you trust your intuition? Are you in tune with what your heart, soul, and mind are telling you? Do you feel confident in the decisions and choices you make? There's more to come on this subject.

Writing

I'm blessed with an amazing life I never thought I deserved, and I believe you deserve an extraordinary life too. I've worked hard along the way as well. One thing that helps me so much is writing things down. We'll talk more about that in Chapter Seven.

I want you to write in this book. I've included lined pages throughout the book for you to write freely. Whatever comes to mind, write it down, even if it seems irrelevant to you. Write down or underline the things that stand out to you. Those notes will be vital to you later. It might even be a significant breakthrough, a key to healing from your past, or a discovery of something new you need to do. Then when you're done with the book, you can go back and reread your notes. I have done this for years, reminding me of what gave me the most help and encouragement.

The following chapters are the ways I've learned not just to survive but to Thrive. That's what I want for you. If this book inspires you with tools, inspiration, and actions to feel like you're Thriving, not just surviving, then I will have accomplished my purpose.

What does it mean for you to Thrive? Let's find out.

Chapter One
WHAT DO YOU WANT?

You're only as happy as you make up your mind to be. —Abraham Lincoln

Do you have things to overcome? Maybe:
shyness
infirmity
anger
overwhelm,
fear
rejection
obstacles
depression
addiction
heartache
grief
loss
trauma
or abuse?

What does it mean to overcome and thrive?

To beat, conquer, defeat, prevail, triumph, get over, get past, succeed, grow, and bloom,
Sounds good.

Hope

Do you feel like life has hit you hard, and you need a little hope? Do you want to know that there will be a light at the end of the tunnel? I'm here to give you hope. You *can* overcome what you're going through or have gone through. I believe you can not only survive but Thrive as well! I have learned to Thrive with a steady diet of a positive attitude, surrender, and exceedingly abundant hope. Right now, I'd like you to start writing what you need to overcome.

What's stopping you from thriving in life?

What do you think is holding you back?

What's frustrating you?

Don't think too hard. Just write what comes to you.

_____

_____

_____

_____

Chapter One

Thrive

Now, what would it look and feel like for you to Thrive?

What would you be doing?

How do you want to feel?

Make a list of your greatest needs, desires, dreams, or goals.

Write fast and don't think too hard. This step changed my entire life. Don't be afraid to dream of big things that seem impossible. Henriette Klauser said in her book, *Write It Down, Make It Happen*, "If you find yourself dismissing a goal as grandiose or far-fetched, write it down and put a star next to it." What would you want to do if money and time were no concern?

So write what you want today, tomorrow, or in your future:

Date:_____

_____

_____

_____

Chapter One

My life changed

The year was 2015 when I did this exercise for the first time. I was cleaning houses for a living, and my figures said I had cleaned 7,000 toilets in 10 years! I loved the work and enjoyed it for a long time but eventually longed for more, like singing for a living. I found a book at a garage sale called, *Write It Down, Make It Happen*. This book **changed my life!** I had written down that I wanted to:

sing in front of thousands of people,

share my story to inspire and encourage women,

quit my job,

write a book, *

be a certain weight,

and deserve to have quiet meditative time studying and reading every day

… to name a few.

Little did I know then that I would accomplish many things I had written down. I'm now a singer, speaker, and author, traveling around the country and sharing my story to inspire and encourage. My husband and I got the opportunity to open for Wynonna Judd! When I started writing this book, I went back to check the correct spelling of Henriette Klauser's name, opened the book to the page I had written all my dreams on, and saw that "write a book" had a star next to it!

I…had…chills!

Chapter One

That was so unfathomable for me at that time. It feels incredible to reach these dreams. That's how I consider myself to be Thriving, not just surviving. But it doesn't make life perfect. As Brian Tracey says, we experience

"problem, problem, problem...*crisis!*"

Life is always throwing us curve balls. That's why I believe so much depends on our attitude and thoughts.

You can accomplish more than you could ever imagine.

"The journey of a thousand miles begins with one step." Chinese philosopher Lao Tzu

Even if it's a step in deciding how you want to *feel* for the day, what would you do if money were no object and time were not a factor? What would you be doing if you had never been through the pain and trials you have experienced or are going through now? Is there a way to find purpose in your pain? If you had died instead of your loved one, *they* would be the one suffering and in grief. You have saved them from that pain. If *I* had not been raped, would I have had a different life? A new friend recently responded upon learning of my rape, "Thank God that you didn't end up sex trafficked like so many young boys and girls are today." I had never thought of that before.

Wouldn't we all love to be free from everything that holds us back: money worries, a frustrating job, an illness? I was initially going to call this book, *Live Free and Die Happy*. I'm a big fan of Bruce Willis in *Live Free Die Hard*. So, I started saying this mantra: "I'm Free to spend as much quiet time reading and meditating every day as I want. And that morphed into "I'm Free to DO whatever I want." It was a new concept for me because of the things we do for love:

The Things We Do for Love

As a woman, it's easy to get lost in motherhood. As a mom, you must push yourself to do many things you don't feel like doing. It all begins with childbirth. You're dying of sleep deprivation, but you must take care of that little bundle of precious joy whose life depends on you. Most of us keep caring for our house and children even when we're sick: cooking, cleaning, wiping noses, and disciplining. Do any ladies agree? As mothers, it's easy to give up so much of ourselves. We can lose who we are inside.

One of my friends went on her honeymoon, and her mother called her when she returned. She asked how the honeymoon went. The daughter replied, "Oh, Mom, the honeymoon was great and wonderful, but as soon as we got home, John started saying four-letter words to me. It's offending me, Mom. I don't know what to do. I'm starting to panic about this. Maybe you should come and get me. I need a break." The mother says, "Well, honey, what on earth is he saying to you? Darling, please tell me". "Oh, Mom, he's saying things like wash, dust, cook, and iron." All the things we *must* do instead of what we want. At least, this has been my experience.

There's a beautiful scene in the movie *Mom's Night Out* where Trace Atkins talks to a worn-out mom who needed a

Chapter One

break and a fun night out, but it doesn't end up very fun. She laments to him, "No matter how much I try, I'm not enough." Trace questions, "Not enough for who?" She answers, "For my husband, kids, my mom, God, everybody... I don't know?" But Trace corrects and interjects, "***You.*** Not enough for ***you.*** It's a beautiful thing watching an eagle take care of her young. It's doing ***only*** what God created it to do. And that's ***enough.*** You all spend so much of your time beating yourselves up. It must be exhausting. God didn't make a mistake when He made you. ***Just be you.*** He will take care of the rest."

I know it's easy to get lost in life, working, living, and surviving in robot mode, and the years fly by. Society tells us we must have all the things, so we work for all the things. Friends or family tells us we should do _____ with our lives... But how often do we take time, be quiet, and listen to our hearts? What would your *soul* guide you to do or *feel* just for today?

_____

_____

_____

_____

_____

_____

_____

_____

_____

_____

_____

_____

_____

The next time someone asks you what you do for a living, and you start to answer, "I'm just a stay-at-home mom." Instead, say, "I'm a research associate in the field of Child Development and Human Relations. I have a continuing program of research in the laboratory and in the field. I'm working on my master's degree and already have four credits (four children).

> *How do you know what your life will be like tomorrow? Your life is like the morning fog—it's here a little while, then it's gone. James 4:14*

Chapter One

If I Die Young

Would dying tomorrow change your today? How about this? What if you were to **die** tomorrow or next year? What would you do today? What would be at the top of your bucket list? That question can put things in a totally different perspective. Now I'm definitely not suggesting we all go quit our jobs tomorrow and just live it up. That question makes me think hard about *what's **important**.* I sometimes think about this question, which helps me with the mundane things I do with or for my children. There can be many frustrating days, **but** when I ask myself this question, it's a joy and honor to be their mother.

*Time and **fun** with my family are at the top of my list.*

I have grandiose dreams, but thinking of dying grounds me in the here and now, and being happy and enjoying what's right in front of me today. I don't need to worry about tomorrow and the what ifs. I trust the sun will still rise.

The more I think of dying tomorrow or next year, the more content I am. I have more patience with my children. I'm more easygoing, laid back, and focused on doing what's vitally important, like writing this book and getting speaking or singing engagements instead of scrolling Facebook or watching TV. Maybe it's being available to talk on the phone with someone having a hard time. It inspires me to live out my purpose to the best of my ability. I wish it were easy to keep focused, but it's not. Is it?

I read daily because I need reminders.

I take time every day to meditate, be quiet, and listen to my heart and soul and what my spirit is saying to me.

I write down what I hear, which gives me the strength to keep going.

That's what I want you to do in this book. I want you to find what the spirit of your soul is speaking to you. I believe you can find your own answers. I believe you'll overcome whatever is troubling you or holding you back.

I was looking up information on knowing what to keep or let go of when moving out of state. I read that you should look around, and if your house was on fire and you only had 30 minutes to grab what items you could, what would they be? Easy…family members, animals, purse, phone, and photographs. At first, I thought this was silly pertaining to moving. Still, it definitely helped with my perspective, as I don't have to *agonize* over every choice and decision. It just means that you have to remember what's truly important: All the **stuff** is not. All the **worry** about the stuff is not worth it.

Life is too short.

So, what would you say if you asked yourself what you would do if you knew you would die tomorrow or next year? Does it help you answer what you want in your life? Write down your thoughts.

Chapter One

Date:_____

_____

_____

_____

_____

_____

_____

Freedom

Do we have the freedom to choose whatever life we want? I'm free. When I started saying this to myself, it released me from self-imposed imprisonment. We do so many things because our family tells us to, the world tells us to, or maybe our bad habits have trained us to do. A homeless man my friend talked to said he didn't want to get a job because he wouldn't have time to help homeless people at the library. He chose to be homeless. We all make our choices and must own up to those choices. But sometimes, things happen to us that **were not** our choices. Those curveballs can take you in a different direction than you had planned; they can get you off course. Trials can trip us up, depress us, and get us stuck in a ***rut*** that we stay in for far too long.

For example, getting raped was traumatic and changed my self-worth, which altered the direction of my life for

Chapter One

many years. I can easily look back on that one event and cry over the lost years of my youth. I could think that if it hadn't happened to me, my life would have been so much better. But I've learned that the "what if" questions never make you feel better. Accepting and moving on with what I have and where I am helps me. What has happened to you that altered the direction of your life? Are we free to *choose* how those alterations affect us?

So to start with, I would say *to love yourself enough* to go through whatever grieving process you need to. We must love ourselves enough to have the courage to accept the things we cannot change, the courage to change the things we can, and the wisdom to know the difference. Understand when you're not in the right state of mind or physically able to make changes. Remember compassion and be gentle with yourself. You might be right where you want to be or in a dire situation you have no control over. What can you do to love yourself today? Write your thoughts. What can you change? Do you feel free?

"If you want others to be happy, practice compassion: If you want to be happy, practice compassion."- Dalai Lama.

_____

_____

_____

AMP Up Your Life

Chapter One

I Deserve

Another thing I started saying to myself is, "I deserve quiet meditative time every morning." Then it morphed into, "I deserve to have what I want, do what I want, and be happy as much as I want." How about you? Do you feel you deserve what you want? Why or why not?

_____

_____

_____

_____

_____

_____

_____

_____

_____

_____

_____

_____

_____

_____

Don't Stop Believing

A baby falls and gets up hundreds, maybe thousands of times to learn to walk. We would never tell that baby to give up. So *don't* give up if at first you don't succeed.

When my husband and I found the house we're in now, it was beyond our budget. It has six and a half acres, which is an absolute dream in this area. Property here's quite costly. We had been looking at homes for one and a half years and were so tired of looking. Our four-year-old daughter kept saying she wanted a two-story house, which my heart also wanted, but I knew we couldn't afford one. We had put in an offer on a short-sale that had 5 acres but was only slightly larger than the current house we were in. We thought that was our only chance for acreage, which my husband wanted, but we also needed a larger home. There was a substantial patch of visible mold in one of the bedrooms, so it required a lot of work. We at least needed a music/guest room, and the short sale provided that. We had put in an offer on the short-sale, and the waiting game began.

During that time, my husband continued searching for homes online. He found a six-acre two-story foreclosure with the roof covered in blue tarp. It was so beautiful. It was a Tudor-style bricked entry. (We both love brick). It was double our current square footage boasting an expansive kitchen with 64 cabinet pulls, and it was open to the family room. And the whole property was completely private. In the meantime, the bank for the short sale accepted our offer, and we had two weeks to decide. We did an inspection which resulted in even

Chapter One

more issues than the mold. How could I settle for that small house when we found an extraordinary dream home? But the dream home was way out of our budget, and we had *no* idea if there was any chance of getting it. My husband wanted to accept the short-sale home, and I didn't. We decided to pass on the first home. We had to give up that good to go for the great. It was an excruciatingly hard decision to make.

So here we were, giving up possibly our only chance for acreage, not knowing the outcome. We bid $50,000 less than asking for the dream home. The bank countered back only $900 less than asking. Our realtor sarcastically quipped, "Are you going to even *consider* countering their ridiculous counteroffer?" She truly made it sound useless. But one of my friends said, "Maybe God wants to give you the desire of your heart?" Those words gave me the courage to try again. So, we countered back a few more times and were able to get it within our budget! Ah, our dream home! We did it. We're here with this big house and tremendous property when we could have just given up.

So, how often do you think we give up in our minds and quit trying, and that's why we fail? Were there times you gave up because you thought it was no use trying?

> *"When you feel you cannot continue in your position for another minute, and all that is in human power has been done, that is the moment when the enemy is most exhausted when one step forward will give you the fruits of the struggle you have borne." -Winston Churchill*

The Reason Why

What are your reasons for doing what you do every day? I'm writing because I've been encouraged by other authors. I want to give **you** hope that you can Thrive no matter what. You're unique and needed in this life. You have a purpose beyond yourself that you can't imagine, more than you could ever dream. I write because my heart has told me to, and I care about you.

> *For although I am free from all people, I have enslaved myself to all in order that I may win as many as possible…becoming all things to all people, in order that by all means I may save some. 1 Corinthians 9:19-23*

Why did you pick up this book? *Why* do you want to Thrive? Write down as many reasons as you can.

Date:_____

_____

_____

_____

_____

_____

Chapter One

_____

_____

_____

_____

_____

_____

_____

_____

_____

_____

"Ask and Receive"

We ask Google, and we receive an answer. Can we get what we ask for in life? There's so much about this topic online. How often do we believe we can get what we truly want? My long years of trials got in the way of my belief. I do know this, if my child really wants something and is willing to wait patiently and continually asks for it respectfully, I will work hard to get it for them. I believe God does the same for us. He loves us so much.

If your child asks for bread, do you trick him with sawdust? If he asks for fish, do you scare him with a live snake on his plate? As bad as you are, you wouldn't think of such a thing. You're at least decent to your own children. So don't you think the God who conceived you in love will be even better? Matthew 7:7-11

Writing down my dreams, aspirations, and even the *way* I wanted to feel opened my life to asking and receiving. So many things I had written down came true. You can ask and receive. Do you believe it? Steve Harvey says, "You must stay on Belief Blvd. Your package only arrives there. If you travel to Doubt Drive, you won't receive it." Of course, we have no idea when the package will arrive. We must have faith it will come at the right time. We must wait patiently and confidently.

Do you believe you deserve good things? I know I didn't for a long time. Dr. Curt Thompson says, "Our trauma, or evil, wants us to forget what we long for." I say that evil wants us stuck in bad thoughts. What do you think about the shooters that go out and kill innocent people? Do you think they have mental issues and wrong ideas control them? I think so. If we keep swirling around the bad thoughts in our heads, we get consumed with them. As soon as we have an invalid belief, we must kick it out as quickly as possible and replace it with a good thought.

You deserve love right now wherever you are. Christine Cain says, "We're crippled by our questions and what if's."

Chapter One

Don't let your past cripple your future. Don't let it take away your belief that you can Thrive and overcome whatever life has dealt you. It's easy to devalue our little bit of time and our little bit of effort. You have much to offer. You're here for a reason. We all need each other. You have something special in you that the world needs. Get up, and do the good thing. Do what you know is right. Don't doubt, and don't stop dreaming!

What do you want?

_____

_____

_____

_____

_____

_____

_____

_____

_____

_____

When time stands still:

When I'm singing for people: time stands still for me. I'm not thinking about the past or the future, but the moment I'm in at that exact time. It's my sweet spot. That's complete and utter *fun* for me. When are you at your happiest? When are you so full of joy that you can think of nothing else? Do you even know what that's like? Think about it for a little bit.

- How about Christmas dinner when you're eating unbelievably delicious food?
- Maybe you like to draw or paint?
- Do you have a hobby you lose yourself in once you start?
- Do you enjoy digging in a garden or reorganizing closets?
- What makes you feel so much better once you get started: exercising, boating, reading, or fishing?
- What's fun for you?
- What do you want to take time to work on today?
- What revives you and gives you energy and rest or inspiration?

Date:_____

_____

_____

_____

_____

Chapter One

_____
_____
_____
_____
_____
_____
_____
_____
_____
_____
_____
_____
_____
_____
_____

Recap:
1. What do you want?
2. Believe you deserve what you want.
3. What's your reason "why"?
4. If you died tomorrow or next year, what would you do today?
5. Remember compassion for yourself and others.
6. When does time stands still?

Amp Up Your Life

Now, what *actions* will you take to accomplish what you want? Transfer this list to your calendar.

Chapter One

Go to our website, Hiscountry.net, and subscribe with your email to receive a free download of our single:

"Don't Give Up"

Hey friends, how is life treatin you
Look at what we've all been going through
Do you know the secrets to a happy life?
Let me know when you get it right.
Simple days, don't we just wish for them.
Trying to keep it all going
Struggles, the world keeps changing.
Constantly need some rearranging.

But don't give up. Don't give in.
Pick up your chin, keep searching for that silver lining
Don't be sad. Just be glad.
Life is too short to worry about tomorrow.

Politics, right or left which area you?
Religion, what looks good on you?
The color of your skin don't matter
We're all in this life together.

So don't give up, don't give in.
Pick up your chin, keep searching for that silver lining.
Don't be sad. Just be glad.
Life is too short to worry about tomorrow.

Amp Up Your Life

Dust off your boots, wipe off your jeans.
Get back on the saddle, take hold of the reigns

So don't give up, don't give in.
Pick up your chin, keep searching for that silver lining.
Don't be sad. Just be glad.
Life is too short to worry about tomorrow.

Chapter 2
A.M.P. UP YOUR THOUGHT LIFE

Sow a thought, reap an action;
Sow an action, reap a habit;
Sow a habit, reap a character;
Sow a character, reap a destiny.
-Samuel Smiles

Everything begins with our thoughts and ends with our destiny. We have thoughts going through our brains constantly. We need to be very aware of the verbal messages we give ourselves all day long. Brian Tracey says, "We are what we think about most of the time."

What do you think about most of the time? How do you feel when you wake up in the morning? Recharged and ready to face the day, or wondering how you can just survive it? Do you ever stop and think carefully about what your mind is thinking? Our brains are always processing something. I love to read, study, and learn self-help, and most importantly, share it with others. I know *I* need daily reminders of how to AMP up my thought life. Our brains are constantly barraged with negativity whether by everyday stressors, news, or the internet.

A is for Attitude

> *Charles Swindoll says, "We cannot change the past, or change how other people act, but we're in charge of our attitudes and how we respond"*

The A in AMP stands for attitude. In psychology, an attitude refers to a set of emotions, beliefs, and behaviors toward a particular object, person, thing, or event. Attitudes are often the result of experience or upbringing, and they can have a powerful influence over behavior.

A distinguishing characteristic of consistently successful people is their ability to maintain a positive attitude. Their mind is *not* taken up with pessimism or negativity. As a result, they focus all their mental energy on exploring solutions, taking effective action, and learning how to get better.

My mom began a small part of my "attitude" journey, but Norman Vincent Peale expanded it immensely with his book, *The Power of Positive Thinking*. A change in a person's attitude will change his or her life.

> *An optimist is one who takes cold water thrown upon his idea, heats it with enthusiasm, and uses the steam to push ahead.*

Chapter 2

Don't we wish we could change the past? Or even more, change what other people do? I went through 15 long years of trials and after such a long time, I thought suffering was normal life. Have you been there? My attitude was pretty negative. I didn't know what it meant to dream. I had a posture of someone weak and unsure.

Life so easily crowds out our dreams, goals, and, more importantly, our purpose. And if you've gone through major trials, it just adds fuel to the fire. It can numb us from that purpose and happiness. Do you feel undeserving of a good life? Do you feel your trials will never subside like waves one after another cashing over you and you can't catch your breath? Another blow when you're already down? Are you drowning and grasping for a way out of the turmoil? Some seasons seem to last forever, but they won't. I'm always encouraged by the words, "It's only a season and this too will pass." Nothing in this life stays the same for very long. Thankfully that includes our troubles.

Just like we need physical exercise to get our bodies in shape, we need mental exercise or discipline to keep our *thoughts* in the best posture or position. As a woman, my mood and mental state can change by the minute. Maybe that's because I'm going through the menopause. It's either that or a mid-life crisis. My mom always said she didn't know why God made us go through menopause at the same time our parents were dying and we had teenagers. It's quite the combination with lots of mental stressors all at the same time. Sometimes life deals us the same cards of trials upon trials.

We can change our attitude. That's *one* thing we are in control of. We don't have to let our circumstances, experiences, or other people's actions control how we feel. I know it's easier said than done. I struggle too. So please don't guilt yourself if you're at the end of your rope with life and don't have a bit of fight and strength in you to work on your attitude. I've been there as well. Take one step at a time and one day at a time. A journey of a thousand miles begins with one step after another. Hold on to hope.

> *Harvard psychologist Williams James said: "The greatest discovery of my generation is that a human being can alter his life by altering his attitudes of mind.*

As a man thinks in his heart, so is he

We must not let discouraging thoughts have one minute in our brain. Kick them out quickly, and as fast as you can. Practice that! The discouraging thoughts will return, but practice replacing them with hope that you can and will succeed and not only survive but thrive. This has been a huge step for me overcoming my past and succeeding in my future. Like the little train that could, tell yourself out loud if need be, "I know I can, I know I can!" For me, this isn't a one-time only accomplishment, but something I have to continually remember and practice. Remember the Little Nemo movie and Darci that said, "Just keep swimming, just keep

Chapter 2

swimming?" She had a five-minute memory, but she could remember that's what she needed to do, swim.

It was an action. Do you *believe* you can overcome and thrive?

A man's life is what his thoughts make of it. Think depressing thoughts and you'll be depressed. Think grateful thoughts and you'll be grateful. —Marcus Aurelius

What's your attitude right now about what you've gone through or are going through? What would you *like* your attitude to be?

_____

_____

_____

_____

_____

_____

_____

_____

Amp Up Your Life

_____

_____

_____

_____

Something I read once was to write yourself a letter of *forgiveness, acceptance and encouragement.* Give yourself love, respect, and comfort like you would a child. When I did this, I felt so comforted!! I forgave myself for being a naïve teenager who made wrong choices. I encourage myself that I can and will do better. If I feel my dreams won't ever come to fruition, I tell myself to trust and not give up, but keep going and keep trying to find something that works. I remind myself in these many different ways to keep on keeping on. I've been stuck in depression before and had no heart or willpower to try anything. I have been there. If you're there, I'm so sorry for your hurt and pain. Feel my arms come around you to hug you and love you right where you are.

Write yourself a letter…

_____

_____

Chapter 2

M is for Mindset.

Whether you think you can or think you can't, you're right. –Henry Ford

Mindset means the habitual or characteristic mental attitude that determines how you'll interpret or respond. How you see and respond to the events of life is shaped by your mindset and patterns of thinking. Therefore, we must train our minds.

Sometimes, it takes a lifetime to learn that what's inside us is valuable and good enough to share with the world. To promote and sell yourself, so to speak, in what you love and enjoy can be quite difficult. I think most of us live with great insecurity. We can have the mindset that we're just so-so, or mediocre.

For quite a few years now my husband and I have traveled doing concerts and speeches. We have received so much positive feedback and comments about how great we are. One group said we were the best music feature they had *ever* had. It has taken years to really believe it intrinsically in our hearts and minds. My husband started playing guitar when he was very young but was told that he could never make it big. We all can make flippant comments (in my case when they laughed at me for singing) that could affect someone, especially a child. Sometimes, it only takes one instance to give us an **incorrect** mindset that sticks with us for years or possibly a lifetime.

Chapter 2

I've been collecting the good comments on our performing and rereading them and believing them in my heart. I've been encouraging my husband and myself, that we *are*, in fact, *good*! We had the amazing opportunity to open for Wynonna Judd, and were told by a friend that she enjoyed our performance more than she enjoyed Wynonna's! With that one comment, I didn't believe it. It was from a friend. But after the fifth friend said the same thing, I finally believed it!

Singing is easy for me, which is why it's hard for me to see it as a special gift. But when I really stop and think about how a singer and song can move *me* and stir in my soul great emotion, then I must have the mindset that I can do the same for someone else as well.

I want you to believe in yourself. Believe in your goodness. You have a unique gift to share. Whatever it is you're struggling with, or have suffered through, you can *thrive*. You may not think what you have is special, but it is.

A friend Tammy Whitehurst said, "***If you're not dead, you're not done!***"

No matter what your age is or what you're going through, my hope is that you find your special gift and share it. Climb out of the pains of your past to a new future of hope. You have nothing to lose do you? Release any self-condemnation and run toward a better future.

Negativity can become a bad habit. Our suffering can keep us in the trenches of hopelessness. Remember that our suffering or evil wants us to forget what we long for.

The Placebo Effect

The placebo effect is when a person's physical or mental health appears to improve after taking a placebo or "fake" treatment. It triggers the body and brain to react as if it's really helping. Belief in a treatment may be enough to change the course of a person's symptoms. Stress is known to increase blood pressure, which, in turn, is a risk factor for heart disease. So, just as the mind can contribute to a physical disorder, it can also contribute to its cure

Remember, in the beginning of the book, I talked about mindset and how we *think* about something has a considerable impact on the results we get. Dr. Alia Crum says, "The placebo effect is a powerful robust and consistent demonstration of the ability of our mindsets to recruit healing properties in the body." In the blink of an eye, we can change any aspect of our mindset.

Take stress for instance. We can look at stress as debilitating and causing anxiety, or we can look at it as a good thing that urges us to get things completed. Dr. Crum said in some studies they did that, "people who *saw* themselves receiving medication, had better physical responses than people who received it *without* knowing." I've been doing dance videos as exercise lately. My mindset believes that it's not as good exercise as what I had previously been doing. But after hearing her talk, I believe I should think of it as just as good or even better because I *enjoy* it so much.

Fear can serve a healthy purpose by reminding us to wear a seatbelt or lock the doors at night. Unhealthy fear leads to anxiety and worry, ending in viselike control. Stress is debilitating and can diminish your ability to think clearly or it increases energy, enhances focus, and heightens alertness. It can take a lot of work to tear down and rebuild your mindset. Practice makes perfect. Think about what you're thinking about and why you're thinking it. You need to AMP up your thought life.

P is for Perspective

Perspective means different ways of regarding a situation or topic: the appearance of things relative to one another as determined by their distance from the viewer.

When you were a child, did you ever lie in bed and peer into the dark and scrutinize in fear over an object in your closet, only to discover it was nothing scary? Our perspective or view of things can easily and quickly change just like that.

Hurricane Irma struck Florida September 10, 2017, ripping off roofs, flooding coastal cities, and knocking out power to more than 6.8 million people, including our home. We had no full power for nine days. (We purchased a generator that powered lights, water, and fridge) Now let me tell you, in Florida in September, it's not the fall season. It's still the heat of summer. Our house was around 100 degrees for those nine days. It was grueling. Trying to function was almost unbearable, and when the power came back on, I thanked God every night for at least a month, that we had power. My perspective on having electricity was immense thankfulness and appreciation. What's so disproportionate now is that it's hard to keep that same perspective. I just take it for granted again.

I can remember my perspective the year my brother was wasting away from AIDS in a hospital bed in our living room. Every day was pain and suffering and great fear. Watching someone you love die a slow agonizing death is truly hell. As a young 21-year-old, I was overridden with guilt because there were moments I wanted him to die so the suffering could end.

My perspective for that year is that a normal, boring day, would have felt like heaven.

I had the blues when I had no shoes, until upon the street I met a man who had no feet

Memorizing this quote from motivational speaker Denis Waitley has helped me tremendously!

How do we keep the perspective of great appreciation? It's so easy to take for granted all the good we have and complain about the mundane little annoyances that come our way. A friend of mine calls one of our frustrations a "first world problem." People who live in third world countries don't have basic needs met like water, shelter, food, or basic medicines. That helps put things in perspective. |We're very privileged and have so much, but can still whine and complain about the silliest things, like slow traffic or not finding your favorite item in the grocery store. We need to try to change our outlook when we have a negative thought about something. When we look *out*side of our immediate situation, we realize things aren't as bad as they seem.

It helps me to remember that nothing lasts forever. I was once watching a little two-year-old running away from his father and remembering my children doing the same thing. It seemed, at the time, that those tiring days of chasing after them would never end, but they did.

AMP up your thought life

Dr. Peale says to never think defeat. "If you feel defeated and think, *I'm tired and weary and I've had it*, that's exactly how it will be. But, if when the going gets rough, you think, *I won't accept this. I will continue to think victory and not defeat*, then all the resources of your nature flow toward achieving victory."

Do you remember the story of the little train puffing his way up the hill saying, "I think I can, I think I can, I think I can?" It really works. When you feel like giving up, give yourself a pep talk and say to yourself, "I can do it. I will keep trying, I won't give up, I will succeed."

It's easy for us to berate ourselves for every little failure, but we seldom encourage ourselves with thoughts or actual words. Have you ever wished your spouse or significant other would encourage you? Give it to yourself in your thoughts or out loud in words.

I think the difficulties we go through help us appreciate the good days. But we tend to forget quickly, don't we? Writing down what you're thankful for is a great place to start amping up your thought life.

When you're in the midst of pain, sometimes, you can't see the forest for the trees. Are you going through something that's stopping you from seeing the forest?

1. What has your attitude been lately?
2. Do you have a certain pattern of thinking that might need to be changed?
3. Can you choose a different perspective and find something good about your situation?

Chapter 2

Chapter 3

ENJOY LIFE: LIGHTEN UP AND LAUGH

A cheerful heart is good medicine. Proverbs 17:22

Do you enjoy life? Would you say that you enjoy every day?

I'm one of those people who are way too serious all the time. I'm always analyzing myself and life and how to work harder and smarter, and I miss the mark on fun. Part of the reason I fell in love with my husband, was because of his wit and humor. We all need to laugh, and I don't come by it naturally, but I have learned a little. Whenever I do actually say something funny, my husband will say, "You made a funny," or I will say it.

I sometimes wonder what funny people do with their brains. Do they always try to think of funny things to say or does it just pop in their heads that way? I'm so jealous of comics. It's a gift.

I saw a sign at the check-out counter of a store in a very remote town. It read: Complaint Department: For service, push the red button (the red button was the center of a mouse trap so if you pushed it, the trap would snap on your finger)

> ***You know you're going to have a bad day when you put your bra on backwards and it fits better.***
> ***Things I learned from my children: A king-size waterbed holds enough water to fill a 2,000-square-foot home, 4 inches deep.***
> ***When you hear the toilet flush and hear the words, "Uh Oh," it's already too late.***

I'm far from graduating from the "laughter is good medicine" class. I have to work hard at reminding my serious self to "Lighten up." I'm a perfectionist at heart. I work hard at doing everything well and I get upset when things *don't* go well.

I know that it's easy to **not** take time to care for yourself or have fun. I generally don't **think** fun. I like to think about work. Accomplishing things makes me feel fabulous.

But I have discovered that when I take some time with a friend or a much-needed break, I come back refreshed and revived and ready to jump back into the saddle. I grew up hearing stories of how my dad used to literally run on the

Chapter 3

job. And I also heard stories that my grandfather did the same. I must admit I did that as well. All I cared about was how quickly I could get a job done, timing myself for each chore. And of course, I made sure I did a quality job as well. But as I have matured, I have discovered that it's nice to stop and smell the roses. It's important to have conversations and get to know people. Sitting and having quality quiet time every morning balances and grounds me. I've heard a wise saying as I'm sure you're familiar with the first half:

> **"The early bird gets the worm……. But the second mouse gets the cheese."**

It just might save your life if you slow down and **enjoy** it. Take time to seek wisdom.

I'm sure you've also heard the flight attendant say that "You must put on your own oxygen mask before putting it on your child." If you're not good to yourself, you won't be any good to anyone else either

I recently told my husband that I need one night a week out to do whatever I want: Whether that's shopping, working on my book, or sitting by a lake to have silence. Boy, do I look forward to that time: It's wonderful. Right now, I'm hiding out in my bedroom to talk with you. Do for yourself what you know will refresh you.

Learn to Let Go

I used to clean my house from top to bottom every week but, having twice as much house now makes it take twice as long. I have learned to let go of some of my perfectionistic cleaning tendencies. Do I like living with dust and some extra dirt? No! But I know that quiet time with myself to read and gain wisdom, time with my husband and children, and time with you, are more important right now. I did let the house go for quite a few years, but now my children are older, and I have them do a lot of the household chores while I direct. They're learning responsibility in the process.

> *Stress Reducer: Put a bag on your head. Mark it "Closed for Remodeling."*

> *God put me on earth to accomplish a certain number of things. Right now, I'm so far behind I will never die.*

> *Life is easier than you think—all you have to do is this: achieve the impossible, do without the indispensable, bear the intolerable, and be able to smile at anything.*

How many times have you had one of *those* days when so many irritating things happen, you just *had* to laugh. Like maybe when you just get done sweeping and mopping the tile floors and you drop a brand new, glass jar of jelly on the tile and it shatters glass and jelly all over the clean floor! So, you go to the store and buy a replacement glass jar of jelly and it happens again a few days later! I just had to *laugh*! I bought a plastic bottle after that. This is a true story.

Chapter 3

We must *look* for the joy. We must hang onto hope, even if we're at the end of our rope. Things could always be worse than what they are. I know for me, when I have certain expectations and they're thwarted, I tend to get upset. It helps me, when I remember to wake up in the morning and feel thankful and to purposefully *enjoy* the day.

What do you think would help you enjoy your days better? Do you think you deserve to enjoy your days? You deserve it. What or who makes you laugh? Are you missing this in your life?

_____

_____

_____

_____

_____

_____

_____

_____

_____

_____

_____

_____

_____

_____

_____

_____

Be Thankful

I'm better than I was, but not quite as good as I was before I got worse.

Do you ever have a Monday when you just don't want to face the day or the world for that matter? I'm having one of those days when I just feel in a funk, and nothing feels right. I have heard countless times that every morning you should write a gratitude journal. List everything you can think of that you can be thankful for.

Lost: Dog with three legs, blind in left eye, missing right ear, tail broken, and recently castrated; answers to the name of "Lucky."

Chapter 3

Rather than give in to a miserable situation, *look* carefully for things you can be thankful for. You can probably see, hear, taste, touch, and smell; your senses would be hard to live without. Do you have a home and bed to sleep in? How about air conditioning or heat? Do you have Tylenol for a headache and Band-Aids with antibiotic cream for a cut? Do you have hot water and a bathroom to use at any time? There's always something to be thankful for.

Look around yourself right now. What are you thankful for?

_____

_____

_____

_____

_____

_____

_____

_____

_____

_____

What is fun for you?

*Follow the impulses of your heart. If something looks good to you, pursue it. But know also that **not** just anything goes; You have to answer to God for every last bit of it. Ecc 11:9*

Compassion

***What do we live for, if it is not to make life less difficult for each other.* –George Elliot**

Accept others' flaws as well as your own.

Studies have shown that when you show and do compassionate acts for others, it enlarges the joy receptors in the brain more than any other thought or act. Empathy refers to our ability to perceive and then feel what another is experiencing. Compassion goes a step further and involves an active wish for an end to that person's suffering. Empathy has an effect on the body that's depleting. It lights up the "pain" regions of the brain, as if we were experiencing the pain ourselves. But compassion has an effect on the body that's nourishing. It lights up the "love" regions of the brain. It causes a release of oxytocin, which then causes a release of dopamine (lighting up the reward center of the brain), and serotonin (which reduces anxiety). My daughter has a very bad cold and cough this week. I know it's miserable when you cough so much that your stomach hurts (empathy). When I want her pain to end, I think about what I can do to help her, and then I do it (compassionate act).

Enjoy life.

Keep Moving

Tony Robbins talks about taking massive action, and I've found in my life that I'm better off when I keep moving in some way, and I don't just mean physically. If you don't know what to do, doing something is better than doing nothing. When you're depressed or down, it's easy to be mentally and physically inactive. Do what you can. Inaction will get you nowhere, but action will get you further ahead than where you are now. One action might be a catalyst that improves other areas of your life.

When I started exercising daily, my body got stronger, and I felt so much better. As a result, I started eating less without thinking about it purposely.

Enjoy life.

Take Care of Your Body

How are you feeling physically? Are you out of shape and you know you should be eating better and exercising? Then do it. Physical exercise strengthens your body, gives you energy, and makes you feel better. Get off the couch and go for a walk. Better yet, call a friend and walk together. Start small if you have to and just commit to 20 minutes every day. Have your workout clothes and shoes ready to go. Plan an appointment time for it. I choose first thing in the morning because I find if I don't, it never gets done. Pick a time you can stick with. Do that for a month and then up your time to 30 minutes a day and up your intensity level. You'll feel a difference. I've been exercising for over two decades, and the times when I haven't been able to, I became depressed so much easier. Exercise is good for your mind. Studies show that exercise is as equally effective as antidepressants; and those have side effects. Don't forget that cleaning the house or doing yard work is physical exercise as well.

Enjoy life.

Get Outside

Being in nature is nourishing for the soul. All the trees and plants give us oxygen. The sunshine gives us Vitamin D. Go look at beautiful landmarks in your area. Pray and meditate. We spend so much of our time looking at screens. Studies show that getting outside in nature:

- Helps your memory
- Makes you feel happier
- Heals your body quicker
- Gives you better concentration
- Prompts weight loss
- Reduces stress
- Strengthens the immune system

Enjoy life.

Chapter 3

Embrace Trials

The Japanese philosophy of Wabi-Sabi describes the beauty to be found in imperfection. The aesthetic is sometimes described as one of *appreciating* beauty that's imperfect, impermanent, or incomplete in nature. It says that decay is as much a part of life as growth. On this earth, nothing lasts, and nothing is perfect. Wabi-sabi gave me acquiescence about my long years of trials. The only people who don't have problems are the ones in the ground. So, problems, frustrations, trials, and sufferings are a normal part of our lives and we should embrace them. Embrace means to hug or hold close to you, to respect, honor or love. I know it sounds strange to try to embrace the bad frustrating things, but it always makes me feel better to think of this when I get upset.

You can inspire people with your flaws and imperfections because that's in our human nature. During a speech I gave, I flubbed my words and mentioned it later to a lady as she was leaving. She said, "Oh that just lets us know you're human."

Embrace and accept life as it is. Tell yourself that problems are normal because they are.

Enjoy life.

Growth

As I look back and reflect on my growth, it has been the greatest when trials or miracles have come, not during the stagnant boring days. When my brother lost his life, I learned a lot about pain and suffering and that some things we just have no control over.

> *Where there's no vision, the people perish.*
> *Proverbs 29:18*

Growth is the process of developing or maturing physically, mentally, or spiritually; to improve and advance. Do you think we all have the capacity to improve?

It seems that all living things grow; plants, animals, germs, and we humans. Plants will grow and *Thrive* with the perfect amount of fertilizer, sunshine, and water. Think about the seed of an oak tree and the many years it grows to tower over us with its shade and strength. We build houses and create paper from trees. They produce and reproduce. It's beautiful.

A baby gestates in their mother's womb. We're born and learn to crawl, walk, run, and talk. Think about all the years we spend growing and changing. What helps us to thrive? Yes, we do physically quit growing at a certain point, but our brains don't ever have to stop growing or learning new things. I think growing our minds helps us enjoy life. When I look back at my life to times when I felt stuck, like I was spinning my wheels not going anywhere; those where times when there was no growth, only stagnation. I've learned in my reading and studying that I must make necessary changes to climb out of a stagnant pit. Sometimes learning new things can be easy but other times it can be quite difficult. Find the things that come easy for you and focus on developing those skills even more. Change is always a constant, and most of us like things to stay constant and regular. It seems easier to maintain a routine when it's the same every day, but we can easily and quickly become bored in a monotonous routine and sometimes need to do something we wouldn't normally do just for fun. Steve Jobs took a calligraphy class for no specific purpose and what came out of that was all the different fonts we now have on our phones and computers. If there's something you've always wanted to try, maybe it's time to just do it.

I think as we get older, too busy, or just caught up in the day to day, we forget to dream and have goals. Taking the time to dream, gives us hope. Dream about what you really want, set some goals, and then plan what steps you have to take to reach those goals. That will produce growth.

A ship in harbor is safe, but that's not what ships are for.

When have you grown the most in *your* life? Do you feel stagnant or stuck right now? There must be one small step you can take to grow. What would it be? Do you think continued growth is important to enjoying life?

_____

_____

_____

Amp Up Your Life

Chapter 3

_____
_____
_____
_____
_____
_____
_____
_____
_____
_____
_____
_____
_____

Enjoy life.

Friendships

Going through COVID showed me how much we need each other. Looking back with perspective and realizing how important something is when you can't have it teaches us a lot. Wasn't it quite depressing not being able to see and be with friends and even family? Companionship brings great joy in life.

Another thing about friendships that I think is important is having several friends you can share your joys and sorrows with to glean comfort, encouragement, and advice or suggestions. Are you taking time to cultivate friendships? I know it can be so hard to make time for it, but for me, it's always worth it. Every single get together isn't always special, but they build on each other and it takes time to get to know each other and open up about life. You're not perfect and no one else is either. Treat them as you want to be treated. Be yourself, be honest, be nice, be encouraging, etc.

The Mayo Clinic says that good friends are good for your health, help you cope with traumas, and encourage you to change or avoid unhealthy lifestyle habits.

If there are people whom you would like to get to know better, ask them. What are your interest? Find people who have the same interests. Ask people you respect or look up to for time to talk. Reconnect with old friends. Take the initiative and don't wait for invitations. It takes persistence to keep reaching out, but I encourage you to keep trying. Go to church, join a club like Toastmasters, volunteer somewhere, or ask a neighbor over for coffee. Get yourself out there and

Chapter 3

don't be shy. We humans all have the same basic needs and are in this world together. We reap what we sow, so be a good friend and I believe you'll get a good friend. Do you have any funny quotes or stories you could write down to remember to share with others to help them enjoy life?

What helps you enjoy life recap:

Laughter
Learn to let go
Be thankful
Compassionate Acts
Keep moving
Take care of your body
Get outside
Embrace Trials
Growth
Friendships

What actions will you take to enjoy life? Make a list:
10 minutes: _____

_____

_____

30 minutes: _____

_____

AMP Up Your Life

_____

One hour: _____

_____

_____

Three hours: _____

_____

_____

One day: _____

_____

_____

One week: _____

_____

_____

Chapter 4
FIFTEEN YEARS OF TRIALS

My mom grew up on a farm in a family of ten children: My dad grew up in a family of six children.

They grew up raising and butchering animals, planting and harvesting a garden along with canning and storing all their produce, and making *everything* homemade! Mom said the only things they bought from the store were things like flour and sugar. We live in a society now that seems so far removed from knowing and appreciating the earth's provisions: the food we eat, the clothing we wear. I have such great respect for the knowledge that my mother has.

Both my parents, Cal and Delta, grew up in the same, small town in Michigan where their families attended a very conservative Mennonite church. The men sat on one side and women on the other. The church did not believe in war. I can remember as a young child, that one of my uncles would not let us girls swim in my grandparent's pond at the same time as the boys. My parents were not *that* strict thankfully. Both families were very nonconfrontational and passive, as in intimidated submissiveness. My mom said everyone knew there was a child molester living in the small town, yet no one did anything about it. I'm not laying blame on anyone. It just hurts my heart so much to think of children who were abused and badly affected by that man. My guess is that was their interpretation of "turn the other cheek." Years later, my mom said that my dad had been molested by him.

In 1965, Mom and Dad had my oldest brother Van. Our last name was Eash, (pronounced esh), so we used to tease him and call him "Vanish" like the toilet bowl cleaner. My brother Dale arrived one and a half years later. When Dale was an infant, his body would bruise with fingerprints where my parents would pick him up! When he was 18 months old, he fell backward off a small riding toy and had a brain hemorrhage. They had to take him to a major hospital two and a half hours away. That's when they discovered he was a hemophiliac. Hemophilia is a disease in which a person's blood doesn't clot normally, so there's excessive bleeding either internally or externally after any injury or damage. Symptoms include many large or deep bruises, joint pain and swelling, and unexplained bleeding. Imagine how hard it would be trying to raise a boy to be careful all the time. What a difficult job that would be, since most boys are always jumping, falling, and getting hurt. Every time that happened, they would have to take him to the hospital to get a shot. He received factor (medicine made of other people's blood) to make his blood clot. Eventually, they were able to give him the shots themselves.

Chapter 4

Here is a poem my mom wrote when my brother was a toddler.

To My Son

Son, we love you very much,
there's nothing we wouldn't do,
to try to help ease all the pain,
this life will put you through.
Many nights I've lain awake
heard you begging again and again,
but all the love I feel for you
could never ease your pain.
I've rubbed your legs and talked to you
till the morning sun would rise,
only to see your pain more clearly
in your sleepy tear-filled eyes.
If I could take the pain you feel,
I never would complain.
There's nothing worse than watching you
when I can't ease your pain.
When I see you with your friends,
and a smile on your face,
I pray that God will help me bear
what will take that smiles place.
For all the fun you've had today,
tonight I'll hear you cry.
I'll rub your legs, we'll talk again
till the stars have left the sky.
You'll have to grab your happiness

and judge it's worth to you.
My love makes me selfish
when I know what you'll go through.
You're so young and full of life
you'll want to run and play.
You and you alone decide
if it's worth the price you pay.

When my brother had his brain hemorrhage, my mom wouldn't leave his side during all the testing and ex-rays they took. He was just a toddler. In haste of the emergency, she forgot to pack her contraception and got pregnant with me. Upon discovering she was pregnant, the doctors suggested an abortion because of the radiation exposure. I'm so glad she didn't listen to them. I was born March 21, 1969.

I have great memories of my younger childhood. My mom taught me much about frugality, and both Mom and Dad were creatively talented. We purchased a used above ground pool, that my Dad put half in ground, and all my summers were full of swimming with neighbors. I loved it!

My mom sewed *all* our clothes that we wore, which I hated as I got older, because other kids had new clothes every year when school started. She had a creative spark when there was no such a thing as Pinterest. She would cut the legs off jeans, sew the leg parts shut and sew on a strap and voila, a purse. She also created a wall hanging with a bunch of jean pockets to hold items. She painted our entire basement floor with fun large stripes. Dad did a tear-out on our kitchen,

Chapter 4

designing and crafting custom cabinets and doors. Never mind that the countertops were orange and the floors were zebra striped!

My mother and father both taught me to sing. Dad would sing at church in a quartet and mom would sing all the time at home. Music is what really connected me to church. I don't think either of them knew how many times I would go sing my heart out walking our ten-acre field and woods.

School was hard for Dale and Mom because he missed so many days or sometimes a month at a time. Mom was deeply offended when the school lied to the Hemophilia Foundation and said they had offered home teaching, when they hadn't.

Mom and Dad had many happy years together when we were young kids. Dad always worked a lot since he was in charge of a hospital lab and on call. But Mom told me in later years that he started disappearing on the weekends and she suspected he was having an affair. As years went by, Dad had a panic attack, because a police officer followed him closely one day, and admitted to Mom that he was **gay** and had been at a gay hangout! Mom was in a state of shock! She told me she had no awareness of homosexuality practices. There was no acceptance or talk on TV about it. I think it took her many years to really believe and accept it could be true. Now years later I find that Mom didn't tell *anyone* what she was going through at that time, not even her four sisters. How terribly sad to go through something so difficult and not have anyone to talk to about it. Mom and Dad stayed together and no one knew their issues. How many people live like that? Did you or your parents?

None of us children had a clue about my parent's marital issues because they hid it well. I remember going to church and thinking they were the *perfect* couple.

Faith is seeing light with your heart, when all your eyes see is the darkness ahead

The AIDS epidemic was in full swing

When my brother was twelve years of age, he came home and told my mom that some of his friends said that they heard on the news that homosexuals and hemophiliacs were both getting AIDS and dying from it. At the time, my mom brushed it off and told him they probably heard wrong. Unfortunately, though, they found it was true. And as fallout from that, the school and friends were very nervous and afraid of him when my brother had any bleeding incidents like a bloody nose. He didn't even have AIDS. The word AIDS then was a death sentence and you didn't dare want to even touch someone with it.

Little did we know that the drug companies that made my brother's medicine knew that it was tainted with HIV, yet they continued to give it to all the hemophiliacs! The hemophiliacs had to play Russian roulette every time they needed their medicine.

My paternal grandfather died in 1982 when I was 13 years old. Then, when I was 14, my cousin's family, were hit by a semi, and my cousin and his oldest daughter were killed

Chapter 4

instantly, while the rest of the family were severely injured except for the baby that had been on the floor of their little pickup truck. We lived near the hospital and my parents had to go identify the bodies. It was scary being so young and seeing the body of a dead little girl at their funeral.

In the summer right after I turned 15, I started riding my bike to town every day (5 miles one way) and would hang out at the arcade, pizza shop.

***Only some of us learn by other people's mistakes;
the rest of us have to be the other people.***

One night, I snuck out to a party where there was drinking. I didn't do anything wrong. I didn't even drink anything. There were two older guys at the party whom I was somewhat familiar with because they worked at the pizza shop. I don't know if it was weeks or months later, but one day in town, they asked me to get into their car and I did. I don't remember why I did or what they said to me. They took me to an abandoned house, and both took turns violently raping me while I screamed "No" for them to "stop." They dropped me off at a friend's house where I changed my torn clothing and went home. I was fifteen or sixteen years old.

Somehow, I got home that day without anyone noticing anything had happened to me. It's kind of strange how some of us can go through these experiences that no one knows of. I shoved away the pain deep down inside.

I became different after that. I don't remember singing anymore. I don't remember too much of the following year.

One remembrance was a white sweatshirt that I created with transfer pictures. I cut off the sleeves and put a fierce looking tiger and lion roaring at each other.

My maternal grandfather had emphysema and used oxygen continually for the last months of his life. Mom was going through very difficult and painful female problems and needed a hysterectomy, but she wanted to wait until he passed away. We had his funeral on my sixteenth birthday in 1985. *Two weeks later,* Mom had her surgery and was in the middle of recovering from it when she received a call from the Hemophilia Foundation. They were notifying us that my brother *had* received medicine that was from an HIV-positive donor. My brother was 18 years old when he was diagnosed being **HIV positive**.

Dale had a girlfriend named Brenda. Brenda's mother was different than anyone I'd ever met. She had long black bouffant teased hair and she would come to her door in the middle of the day with thick fake eye lashes and very tiny seductive black lingerie that left little to the imagination. She was usually very friendly and giddy, but when they found out about Dale being HIV positive, she and her older son, who had done prison time, came over and threatened our family harm if we didn't stop my brother and Brenda from seeing each other. Fortunately, they didn't follow through with the threat when they continued their relationship.

A year after my grandfather's death, my maternal grandmother had a stroke and needed 24-hour care which my mother helped out with, 45 minutes away.

Chapter 4

When my mother was going through what I call hell with my father, her female problems, burying her father, caring for and watching her sick mother pass away, and the stress of a son who could die from AIDS, I gave her such a hard time as a teenager. I would yell and fight with her until I got my way. I just wanted what I wanted all the time. I demanded and begged and pleaded to go out at night. I'm so sorry I treated her so badly those years. I had no idea or comprehension of the pain she was suffering from or the grief she was experiencing.

I don't have all the answers to how much we should share with our children, but I do wish I had known more of what she was going through. That's probably why I'm more open with my children about my feelings.

I recall Mom driving an hour away to the nearest mall and wondering why on earth she went, when I knew she detested shopping with a passion. Years later I found out she was seeing a counselor in that area and just needed the respite from all of us. I don't know how she survived it all. But she did survive and is the best mother ever. I'm so thankful for her perseverance and never giving up on me.

I had an STD from the rape and had no clue what it was until I found a book from the library that described it. We didn't have Google back then to look things up. It was crabs or pubic lice. I had no idea what to do about it. A year later I ended up dating a boy, Brian that had quite the reputation for getting in trouble at school and I got pregnant!

My mom was working for an OBGYN doctor at the time. He seemed like a very sophisticated, upstanding Christian who attended our church. When Mom took me to get the pregnancy checked, I broke down with everything in me, to tell him I had crabs. I was so ashamed and embarrassed. He told me that there was nothing I could do about it. I believed him. I never told my mom about it. Shortly after, Mom and I got in a huge fight, she kicked me out, and I moved a couple hours away with the boyfriend's family. Then, unfortunately, their three-year-old son got crabs, so we all had to be treated! I had no idea it could be spread to others.

How embarrassing it is to say all this. Do I really want to share this truth with you all? Absolutely not! The only reason I share these awful details, is because there's usually a reason people make mistakes or get into trouble. I'm not saying excuses. I'm saying there are usually circumstances, situations, and upbringing that they don't have any control of. We must look past the mistakes and see a child, a person who longs for love and acceptance; not judgment. Please don't judge. Give love and compassion. What's on the outside is just a small piece of the puzzle. No one has walked in another person's shoes through every good and bad day of their lives. There's so much more to someone's story than what you see now. I'm not saying to *trust* everyone, just give love. Give what you can.

I used to think everyone experienced such adversities like I had, but they don't. Many people don't understand how hard it is to shake the dust off the effects of those tribulations.

Chapter 4

I have always struggled with insecurity, and it has taken me many years to truly believe that I deserve happiness and goodness and love.

So, I had my first son at seventeen years old. That was the first, *best* moment of my life. November 10, 1986, my son Dane, was born. I loved being a mom, so I began my love of reading nonfiction self-help books like James Dobson's books on parenting. Thankfully, I was set to graduate early, so I only needed a few months of night school to get my diploma. Brian and I got married, of course, and life went on. I found a job as a nanny for an amazing sweet Catholic family with three children. The dad, Bill, taught me how to cook and the mom, Mary, taught me how to clean, which also served as a great income for many years later in life. What fun memories we had together

Reflect on your own life. Have there been trials or traumas you've gone through that you haven't told anyone about? Do you have someone you could talk to about it now to get it out in the open? Are there things from your past that you're still bitter about or have never healed from? How do you feel about these experiences, and how do you **want** to feel?

_____

_____

_____

_____

"Brother Where Art Thou"

Matthew 5:3-5 Blessed are the poor in spirit, for theirs is the kingdom of heaven. Blessed are those who mourn, for they shall be comforted. Blessed are the meek, for they shall inherit the earth.

AIDS

During his senior year, my brother Dale and I would go to The Skate Place where they had dancing only on Saturday nights. Dale was an amazing break dancer, and people would gather in a huge circle around him while he popped and locked and did the spin on his spine on the floor. I wish so badly I had video of him but there was no such thing as a cell phone video camera then. He was very talented.

Chapter 4

AIDS invaded our lives and there was nothing we could do about it. My brother was HIV positive. What did I think about this? I don't think I comprehended, at 16, how grave this disease was. Dale was the first AIDS patient in our county. He started getting sick, but he desperately wanted to go to college, get a job, and live a *normal* life. He went to college for denture making and pushed forward, even though he always had a fever the entire time he was in school. In the meantime, he and his girlfriend got pregnant and they had a little girl. But, of course how dreadful and terrifying for my mother to know that his wife and daughter could have or get AIDS as well. Dale was so happy to be a daddy and feel the love you have for your child. He graduated and got a job, but only lasted a few months before he got too sick to work any longer. The Hemophilia Foundation talked him into taking AZT, the only medication they had come up with for AIDS patients. Unfortunately, two weeks after he took it, he became bedridden and never recovered.

My father was a homosexual, yet, my brother, who was straight, got AIDS!? So ironic, don't you think?

Shortly after Dale moved back home, they had to get a hospital bed for him to put in the corner of the living room. Mom asked Brian and I to move back in with them because she needed help caring for Dale. Mom worked the afternoon shift, and she would come home and find Dale hungry and had not been given his medication. So there were eight of us living in the house together then; My mom, Dad, myself, my husband, our 4-year-old son, my brother, his wife and their

2-year-old daughter, Hope. I was in charge of the laundry and cleaning, and Mom was in charge of dinners and Dale's round the clock medicines. I will never forget looking at his medication list and wondering how on earth my mother kept it all straight. Thankfully she was a nurse and knew much more than I did about how to do it. I was thankful that my parents were in the medical field, although I had no desire to follow suit. I really don't remember Dad doing much to care for Dale. Dad had always been a workaholic, or so I thought at the time, and continued to bury himself in his work. Dale's wife chose the path of disappearing as well, for she was always going to town to do something. I think it was just their way of escape and running from the pain of watching him waste away. But it became very grueling for me and Mom to carry the day-to-day burden of care.

The perpetual smell of bleach hung in the air as we had to wash all our dishes in it. My brother had terrible mouth sores and he had to gargle and swish with a prescribed lidocaine mouthwash just to numb his mouth enough to be able to eat. Eventually, the sores in his mouth became so bad that the doctors told my mom to keep towels near the bed at all times because they could eat a hole into a vein, and he could bleed to death. His medications had to be administered every four hours around the clock and when he could swallow no more, they had to be inserted rectally. What this meant was that my mom did his last evening dose at midnight and set an alarm for his next dose at four am. This continued day after day, and week after week. Dale talked to mom one grave

Chapter 4

late evening and said "Oh Momma, I know you love me so much, but you're getting so tired. I am so tired of living."

During the arduous year, I found a notebook of Mom's that I started reading, and discovered that my dad was gay! I was completely shocked. But with so much going on, I didn't have time to think about it and just shoved it deep inside.

At church, people said to Mom, "If you have enough faith, he will live." How could they say something like that to her about a disease that *no one* survived from? I'm sure they were just doing their best to encourage her with hope, but it only hurt her deeply.

It was March in Michigan and the days of winter were oh so long and we always craved to see and smell spring in the air. The barren trees completely stripped of any vegetation would *eventually* sprout very small chutes of green leaves. Dale desperately longed to see spring begin before he died. He held onto that hope through the depressing long winter and the pain and agony he felt daily.

As a naïve young woman, I never took the time to express to him how much I loved him. As the agonizing months persisted, I was very ashamed of the feelings that I wished all the suffering could be over. I wished he would pass on, so the nightmare would end. Hospice (a medical agency that helps people with end-of-life care) was such a blessing to us as we could share our feelings of sadness and grief of the process. They understood and said it was normal to feel that way.

It was April 21 of 1990, and Mom asked my dad and I to go to town and pick up a few groceries. We were only in the store for a few minutes when they announced over the loud speaker (before cell phones) for Cal and Deanne to come up to the counter for a phone call. We both knew he had probably passed away. Mom said to come home and we learned that Dale had taken his last breath. My brother was gone. His pain and suffering ended. Ironically, the waiting for spring came suddenly. During the viewing at the funeral home it was over eighty degrees. I remember my mom *not* crying at Dale's funeral, and realizing that she had shed many tears before that day, for she knew that day would come.

I'm going to share excerpts of a letter my mother wrote and sent me after we had discussed how she must have shed so many tears during Dale's illness.

I am thinking back to how this particular traumatic day started. The day was a quiet normal day. I began the normal housework that needed to be done. I went downstairs to the boys' bedroom to get laundry. I didn't go into their bedroom often, it was such a mess and mostly I just let it be a mess. This particular day, the floor was covered with clothes and the bed was a pile of blankets. As I looked around and assessed the situation, I saw a wall hanging of Jesus on the Cross at the head of Dale's bed. Then I looked at the foot of his bed and there was a statue of Jesus with his arms outstretched. It was a glow in the dark statue.

I suddenly realized that every night Dale lay down to sleep with Jesus surrounding him. And that every time he opened his eyes, the first thing he saw was Jesus with his arms outstretched welcoming him. I then realized Dale accepted his illness and death in a way I could not.

What happened next is hard to explain and painful to my heart. I fell to my knees in that pile of dirty clothes. I began screaming at God. I pounded the rumpled bed. I said a lot of things to God, in the midst of my screaming. I told Him I hated him, and He was not fair. My son did not deserve to be sick. I told God I would not let Him have my son. I pounded my chest and screamed he was mine.

When Dale stopped breathing, I would share my breath with him. When his body was cold, I would wrap myself around him and keep him warm. I would keep my son for myself. My son belonged to me. The thought came to me that God may hate me and strike me dead. After a time of sobbing into the pile of dirty laundry, I was exhausted. I became quiet and waited for God's anger. But instead, the room became peaceful and quiet; a special aura of understanding. What was this? I realized God could handle my anger and grief. I felt Him hugging me with peace and comfort. I sat a long time in the rumpled dirty room enjoying God's love.

And life continued in its tangled way. It was a turning point in my understanding. I fought with God and He still loved me. God and I became better friends. I was aware of HIS terrible pain and suffering at giving His son for us. We talked a lot after that. I realized I didn't have to be in an attitude of kneeling prayer to talk to Him.

***God's brilliance shines best on shards of broken glass.
Delta Eash Partlo***

For me, the year that followed Dale's death, was one of shock, depression, and grief. I was in a fog of emptiness and heartache. Anyone who has ever lost a loved one knows the fog you walk through for many drawn out months. I would look at strangers and wonder what pain and suffering *they* may be going through. There are so many facets to each of our stories that we're unaware of.

Mom and Dad got a divorce just a few months after Dale died.

Several years later, Mom went on to work for hospice: A medical agency that helps people with end of life care. Here is a poem my mother wrote after working with hospice for many years:

"A Hospice Workers Prayer"

Give me strength, Father
Keep me awake,
One more mile
For Jesus' sake.
Hold me up
Keep me aware,
While I try to bring comfort,
To deaths cold stare.
Keep me from drowning
In the river of tears,
I swim through
In my final years.

Chapter 4

> Watching the terror
> In dying eyes
> As they plead for mercy
> To avoid death's surprise
> I walk daily
> Through the valley of death,
> Waiting and waiting
> For the last gasping breath.
> Give me strength, Father,
> Give me joy,
> So I can keep walking
> This dark valley below.
> It's a hard job
> You've asked me to do
> I need your strength
> To keep working for you.

Have you lost someone? Have you suffered trials that left you in a fog of brokenness and despair? Are you there now? Again, write a note of encouragement to yourself to overcome and thrive in spite of that tragedy. You can overcome and Thrive in spite of it all. I believe you can.

_____

_____

_____

It's so hard to fathom all my mother went through in that 10-year span of time: Her husband's infidelity, the fear of

Chapter 4

AIDS, her teenage daughter becoming a mother, the heartache, sadness and loss of her parents and son. My mother deserves a medal of honor.

But, new joy came into our lives again as I got pregnant with our second son, Dillon. All I cared about was being the best mom I could be to my children and the best wife to my husband. It seemed my husband was *never* happy, though. Nothing and no one was ever good enough for him. He was always dissatisfied with his job or me. I thought it best if I shoved my problems and feelings deep down, just like I had everything else. I lived a very sheltered life. Most of those years, I had no personal friends or outside activities beyond my nanny position.

But my husband, Brian's verbal abuse started getting worse. He drank a lot when he was home. It seemed he didn't know how to stop drinking once he started. Brian worked construction and had to travel a lot and was gone during the week. I remember begging and pleading him for money for bills and food, which he was very reluctant to give me. I made $80 a week at the time as a nanny, so it wasn't much to pay bills with, but it seemed he expected us to survive on my income alone. One weekend, I was cleaning out his jeans pockets and I found a receipt. It was from a restaurant and the total was $100 for two entrees and alcoholic drinks for he and his buddy. I was astounded at that price tag; that he would spend that much money on *one* night when I so desperately needed the money for bills. He would get his paycheck and just spend without any concern about bills. Then there were outbursts of anger and punching a wall or kicking the dishwasher. As the years went by, the drinking, outbursts, and verbal attacks continued to escalate.

There were so many nights of one-way ranting and berating me. It was the same every night about how hard he worked and how dumb his boss was and how all of his problems were something or someone else's fault. I never argued, just listened, taking the brunt of his frustrations as all the complaining slowly chipped away at my soul. He complained about me. "Why can't you go get a better job and make more money?" "Why can't you lose weight and get in shape?"

Meanwhile, his drinking and angry outbursts continued to worsen. I was running a daycare out of my home by then and one night he stayed up late drinking, and left fifteen to twenty beer cans on the coffee table and floor, and passed out on the couch. I accidentally woke up late to my first mom dropping off her child and as she entered, she saw all the beer cans and him sleeping! So I wasn't surprised when she came to pick up her daughter and told me her mother would be watching her from now on. I was upset that I had lost that family because of his drinking, but it never occurred to me to ask him to quit drinking. I was living my life out, as my parents had showed me. Never confront what's bothering you: Shove feelings deep inside, and hide everything.

Brian's friends were hinting to me that he was having an affair and when I confronted him about it, he denied it, and I believed him. The next thing I knew was that he had plans for us to move to Arizona and live with his Aunt. We sold everything we owned and left, much to my mother's sadness. Why couldn't I have realized at the time that he was probably running away from his affair to escape the mess he had made? And why didn't I realize that I could have said, "No, I don't want to go?"

On our drive to Arizona, he suggested that I could make good money as a stripper! It seemed all he cared about was making lots of money, or get rich quick schemes. We arrived and were welcomed by his Aunt Dottie. Brian found a job, and I enrolled our first grader, Dane in school and took care of his two year old brother, Dillon. Brian became very angry with me because I wasn't going out and getting a job. All I could think about was, "How am I going to go out and find a job when I had no car and had a two year old to take care of? How did he expect me to do this?" So every night after dinner he would scream and yell at me about it. He was mad that I wasn't going out to find a job, especially a stripper job like he had suggested. He would scream and rage for an hour or two every evening. Finally, Aunt Dottie said she needed to talk to us about something. She calmly and assertively announced, "The yelling and screaming will not be accepted in my house. It will stop or you'll have to leave."

Movin' On

So, naturally, we left and moved to Corona, CA, an hour east of Los Angeles, where Brian found a job making good money doing horizontal earth boring under streets and roads. We rented a condo and lived there with no beds or furniture of any kind. I stacked cardboard boxes in the closets to put our clothes on. But things seemed promising because it was a good job, and it was a beautiful place to live.

Just a few months later when we thought things couldn't get better Brian got laid off for the winter! We were astounded. We understood that in Michigan, where they had winter, but California didn't have winter. We were out of options, so Brian called his brother Greg who lived in San Diego and asked if we could move in with them. I wish so badly I would have suggested we just go back home. Maybe I did and I don't remember. We broke our lease and moved in with Greg, his wife, and two children. Weeks turned into months of no work.

Finally, tensions were rising with our living arrangements and somehow my Dad drove all the way from Michigan to California to pick up the boys and I. Brian had just returned to his job so he stayed behind. I don't remember how this transpired. I think I've blocked out so much of the pain. Dad must have sensed something was deeply wrong. The boys and I didn't have much when we got back home in Michigan. I remember eating peanut butter and jelly sandwiches every day for lunch for a month. I found a job working at a barn retail store but it didn't last long. Then I got a waitressing job at a restaurant. I started out on a midnight shift and I would work all night, get home, send Dane to school, and then try to sleep on the couch while Dillon, who had just turned four, played. One day I woke up at noon to see Dillon sitting at the table trying to cut an apple with a steak knife. I immediately

Chapter 4

went to work and explained I needed an afternoon shift and, thankfully, got it. But that also meant that my mom would work all day at her nursing job and then come home to watch the boys so I could go to work.

It was the evening of June thirteenth, 1994 and we were celebrating Dillon's third birthday. I noticed an unfamiliar car pull in the driveway and much to my surprise, I watched Brian step out. He hadn't told me he was coming back! After everyone left, I questioned him about the car. He had purchased it from a used salesman and had written two postdated checks as the down payment. He brought *no* money back with him! I said, "Why couldn't you have stayed and worked another two weeks and had made $2,000 to bring back?" Inside I was boiling that he came back with no money! He did find a job. He was always good at finding jobs, but I was still upset that he had returned unprepared. I had enjoyed being without him for a month. Many nights he would go out drinking and one night I said, "I want you to stop drinking for a month." It was the first time in our marriage that I told him what to do or at least told him what I wanted. I had been reading relationship books for years and had given up on changing him and realized I had to change myself. I was getting stronger, and somewhat learning how to get my feelings out.

The reprieve from his manipulative and controlling ways helped me gain strength to speak my mind and moderately begin to realize I was a person who deserved to be heard and respected. One evening, he had a long and exhaustive tirade about life and me and everything. I was so tired and worn down from listening to his hour long rant. It wore me to a frazzle.

It all came to a head that night when we got in bed and I talked *back* to him for the first time in our marriage. He would be leaving the next morning to go to his construction job and be gone all week and he wanted to have sex. I said, "If you think I'm going to do that with you, after all that yelling and complaining you just did, you can forget it." He went ballistic! In a fit of rage, he grabbed the bedroom door and ripped it off its hinges and hurtled it across the room. He pounded his fists and tore massive holes in the drywall. He tipped over a very wide and tall heavy bookcase full of collectables. He did this while he yelled and screamed things my brain has blocked out. I was terrified for my life. Looking in his eyes was like seeing a man demon possessed. I was terrified that he might hurt me and I was sure the boys on the other side of the wall were terrified of what was happening. Calmly sitting on the bed, I tried to tell him we needed to separate and get counseling, but that only made him worse, so I kept myself calm and pretended nothing was wrong. I pretended I wasn't scared. I pretended that everything was okay so that he would calm down and end his tirade that went into the early morning hours.

The following day, I gingerly brought up counseling again, and he, in his customary manner, came up with excuses why he didn't need it. "Counselors aren't perfect, and they don't know anything." After he left, I had my parents

Chapter 4

come over and showed them what he had done and I told them I was leaving him for good. I fled in hiding with the children to that wonderful Catholic family's home. I hadn't worked for them for quite some time, but they took me in for a week, even with worries that he might try to find us. Upon entering, Mary looked at me and said "Oh my, Dee, you look like you're 40 years old." At that time I was 26. I got an attorney, a restraining order, and started to process for a divorce.

Fortunately for me, my ex-husband fled to California shortly after. When he left, I was so happy to see life out from under his controlling and domineering ways. At my job, I saw a new life I never knew existed with people and laughter. I had led such a sheltered life most of those years with no friends to confide in, and stayed away from church because my ex had said they were all hypocrites. I forgave myself and Brian for the mistakes we made. We both came from trauma and abuse.

We couldn't afford much. Many times, our dinner would consist of the three of us sharing one can of vegetable soup. Dinner at McDonald's was about a once a month treat. I was a very hard worker and felt an enormous amount of stress trying to raise the boys on my own. In 1997, four years after my divorce I decided I wanted to go to college to make something of my life. I wanted to be a counselor. My first semester, I received a 4.0 GPA. What I enjoyed the most was a Beginners Voice class when I sang "My Heart Will Go On" by Celine Dion. It was an out of body experience singing onstage in front of people for the first time. Mom and Dad were there and Dad said, "I can't believe you did that!"

My mom mentioned that there was a special three day revival series at the church, so I decided to go. The pastor, Jay Carty, who was visiting from California said, "If you don't remember asking Jesus into your heart as the most pivotal moment of your life, then you haven't done it and you need to." So that day I stood up and asked Jesus into my heart. And, I started praying and talking to Him on my drives to and from college.

I was coming to the end of myself. God was working on me. I knew I wasn't living right. I hadn't been in church in eight years. My relationship with men was so skewed. I didn't know how to say no to them. It was like I was stuck in my 15 year-old body that was screaming "no" for the rapists to stop, but feeling no power or thought on how to make it happen with a boyfriend.

I started a journal for the first time since I was a teenager and wrote on the first line, "This is going to be the truth and the truth is finally going to come out." By writing the truth, I saw who I really was and the truth of my actions, and I didn't like what I saw. I was promiscuous, and occasionally going out to a bar and drinking, and I was dabbling with marijuana. That truth was on paper, and my mind couldn't deny it easily anymore.

One day, lying on a blanket in the soft grass in May of 1998 in my backyard, I spread my arms out as if on the cross with Jesus and gave myself over to Him. I wanted to die with

Chapter 4

Him. I confessed, "I can't be in control of my life anymore. I want you to take *complete control* of my life. Do anything you want to me or through me. I just want to be a good person and help people."

Two weeks after that prayer, I had a major nervous breakdown! I flipped out. The new friends who had moved from Chicago that I hung out with from work had mentioned the word "cocaine," which scared this smalltown girl. I caught them trying to sneak into my house, and I assumed they were going to steal from me. Later on at work, I said to one of them while he was working behind the bar in front of quite a few people, "You're gay and you have sex with boys." Don't ask me why I said this to him. I just felt at the time that it was true and I was letting out my anger over all I had been through in my life and feeling like he and his friend had tried taking advantage of me. I left and called 911 because I was paranoid that they were going to try to kill me. I'm sure the poor dispatcher I spoke with assumed I was a nut-job. I remember small parts of the conversation when I started ranting about my displeasure with my dad and our lives. The police came and graciously followed me home after I begged them to, but I drove down the road to my mom's house instead. I was in a complete state of paranoid anxiety. I was cookoo for cocoa puffs. I ended up staying there for a week. At the time, my boys were visiting their dad. I tried going back to work, but I just couldn't do it.

My step dad took me to the police station and I reported to them about the talk of cocaine, who was involved, and about being raped. They gave me a number for a rape counseling agency.

I was hearing voices in my head and my mind was playing tricks on me. One day, sitting at Mom's kitchen table, I was overcome with the thought that my stepdad wanted me sexually, even though he hadn't insinuated that in any way. Then I became terrified that he wanted to kill me, because he was sharpening his long carving knife. I stood up and started frantically reciting the Lord's Prayer out loud.

"Father who art in heaven, hallowed be Thy name, Thy kingdom come, Thy will be done, on earth as it is in heaven. Give us this day our daily bread and forgive us our debts as we forgive our debtors. And lead us not into temptation but deliver us from evil. For Thine is the kingdom, the power, the glory forever. Amen"

I said this a few times, and, instantly, the fear that had gripped me vanished. Although healed instantly in that moment, I returned home by myself in a state of deep dark depression. After I went back home, I was standing in my bedroom and suddenly had such a vivid flashback of the rape; it was as if it had just happened: The abandoned house, the tall unkempt grasses and shrubs shielding the view of anything around us, laying on my back in the front seat screaming "No stop," as they took turns raping me ripping my pants in the process. The feelings and memory was just as intense as it was that day it happened. For a few weeks, voices in my head were telling me what an awful person I was. I was a mess. I felt like God body-slammed me in a boxing ring,

Chapter 4

and I was down for the count. For the first time in our lives, I divulged to my dad on the phone that I knew he was gay, and I still loved him.

I'm so thankful that my mom was a nurse. She started me on an antidepressant called Wellbutrin that was particularly to help people quit smoking. I had been smoking since I was sixteen, a habit I picked up from my dad and a girlfriend who talked me into it. All the years I was single mom, I smoked *two* packs a day! I have always been an instruction reader, so the instructions said to pick a stop date to quit smoking, and I did. June 30 1998 was the day I quit smoking and I never picked up another cigarette again. That was the day I started jogging every day.

I went to the rape crisis center and got some wonderful group counseling guided by an instrumental workbook. But, what healed me the most was reading my Bible every day, all day long. The boys came back from their dad's and I would send them to school and read that Bible all day. Slowly, my depression lifted. The voices went away. God gave me *time*: Time to *grieve* everything: my rape, my brother's death, my dad's secret life, my divorce, and my lack of control over my own life. I'm so thankful I had two parents who supported me mentally, physically, and financially during that healing time.

My favorite verse that I found and clung to was John 12:27. At the time Jesus is in the garden of Gethsemane praying because He knows He is going to be sacrificed the following day. So, He prays this prayer, "Now, my heart is troubled, and what shall I say, 'Father save me from this hour?' No, it was this very reason I came to this hour, Father I glorify Your name." He was willing to go to His death, and trusted His Father God. That's what I clung to, that I could trust my heavenly Father with *my* life as well: my painful past and suffering; and to trust Him with my future.

It's so hard to share these details, but I write them to encourage you that you can make it. You'll be okay. I've learned to watch for my signs of depression and have learned how to quickly do whatever it takes to get back on track. Your self-care is so important. I will talk more about this in a later chapter on Depression.

> ***The events of our lives, when we let God use them, become the mysterious preparation for the work He has prepared us to do.***

What does my story stir up in you?

_____

_____

_____

_____

_____

_____

Chapter 4

Chapter 5
A FAIRY TALE NEW START

Two months later, I got a phone call from my Aunt Hannah (my dad's sister), "Hi Dee, would you want to go out double dating with me and Dennis (her husband) and his brother Duane, who is up on vacation from Florida, to a Chinese restaurant and putt-putt golfing?" I said, "Sure," before I could think of a reason to say no. The day came, and we went out and had a good time. I didn't pay too much attention to Duane, because I was busy talking to my Aunt Hannah who I didn't get to see very often. Four years earlier she had married Dennis. They both were in their forties, neither had ever been married, they both lived with or near their mothers, and they lived in the same small town with one blinking stop light that my parents had grown up in. I grew up forty-five minutes away. Dennis's brother, Duane, sang at their wedding, and I had just recently gotten divorced at that time.

Duane had moved to Sarasota, Florida with a cousin after college. Later, I found out that on a few different trips back up to Michigan, he had tried finding me at work or at home with no luck.

It was a beautiful sunny summer day in August of 1998. My mom, stepdad, dad (yes, they got along), grandmother, and my boys, were all in the front yard when we got back from our date that Saturday in August. They were soaking up the warmth, sitting in the soft green grass on blankets and lawn chairs. You cannot do that in Florida with the biting red ants, but in Michigan there are no red ants and you can lie in the grass if you want. It's always the first thing I do when I go back home.

I wasn't purposely playing hard to get that day, but I remember trying to hide the fact that I thought this guy was so big, strong, and handsome. I went into the house and he followed me using the excuse, "I need to use the bathroom." He came out just as I was ready to go back outside. He asked, "Would you like to go out again tomorrow and ride the train with the boys? I said, "Yes," again. The next day, he presented me with a pretty single yellow rose, which, of course, I thought was so sweet. The boys and I enjoyed the train ride, which we had never done before. That evening, he came to my house and we sat around a campfire with the boys. Duane had brought his guitar and started playing. He was *so* good. But what truly amazed me was when I would mention any song and he could just play it by ear. Any song! I was pretty impressed to say the least. That probably did me in. He wooed me playing his guitar.

Chapter 5

He left the next day, and so began our long-distance relationship. We talked on the phone many nights until midnight. He had a cell phone back when you were charged by the minute and had some hefty phone bills! One night, right after we got off the phone at midnight, my ex-husband's wife called me to ask about our relationship. She said, "Brian has been beating me and I have pictures of bruises all over my body." I'm still not sure why she called me. Probably just to confirm that he had been abusive to me as well. I felt so bad for her and thankful that I ended the relationship when I did. I think she needed confirmation, but I got it as well.

Duane and I emailed each other back when my old computer still had dial up and made this awful screeching sound as it started. Email was all I had or knew how to use. There was no such thing as Google, Facebook, or the world-wide web yet, at least not in my realm of life.

Duane invited me to Sarasota for a week. My mom so graciously kept the kids, telling me, "You're going to have such a good time." I kind of wondered how she knew that. I think she knew he was an answer to a long-awaited prayer for me. It was helpful that our families grew up in such similar ways and had known his family all our lives. It had been a long four and a half years as a single mother. One of the most challenging things for me, was not being able to fix all the things that quit working, or the windows the boys broke playing baseball. The unruliness and anger of my oldest son was heartbreaking. The stress of trying to survive and be a mom and a dad to my boys was huge. I desperately wanted to be a good mother.

I stepped off the plane in my business casual dark blue blazer and I couldn't help but melt inside, when his eyes lit up seeing me. He tried to come and hug and kiss me, which took me by surprise. I pushed him away teasingly as if he shouldn't be doing that. I wasn't ready for that yet.

We spent most of the week just talking and driving around seeing the incredible beaches, palm trees, and beauty of the area. At his apartment, he played his *keyboard* for me and impressed me *again* with a different instrument and his gift for playing by ear. He was big and strong, yet gentle and steady. He was kind and caring and great at dealing with people. He was so different than my ex-husband, who was so wild, spontaneous, and seemed to think that life was only about him. Duane cared about whether *I* was happy and comfortable. We became so close in that short week, but I casually told him, "I have to have a commitment: This had to be a sure thing." I still can't believe I even said that. Then I went back home from that sunshine state as happy as could be.

Popping the Question

A few months later he came back up to visit me again and took me out to the same Chinese restaurant where we had our first date. I ordered Szechuan chicken not realizing that it would very spicy and I didn't want to let on that my mouth was on fire! I excused myself to the restroom to take

Chapter 5

a breather, and when I came back, he handed me the fortune cookie, and as I opened it and pulled out the paper, it said, "Will you marry me?" and Duane was on his knee with a huge diamond ring in his hand! My heart melted, and, of course, I said, "Yes!"

We were married soon after that. Neither of us wanted to wait. We sang, "From This Moment On" by Shania Twain, to each other at our wedding. We knew that God had brought us together and we were sure about that and that fact has kept us going through thick and thin.

Duane asked me if I wanted him to move back to Michigan or if I wanted to move to Florida, and I said, "Palm trees and the orange state? Are you kidding me? Let's move to Florida." I couldn't wait to get out of the cold and away from so many painful memories to a fresh new start. I flew to Florida again and we found just the right house for us to buy and start our lives together. Our married life began December 31, 1998 during the snow in Michigan and then on to an amazing honeymoon in Hawaii. I felt like I was in heaven. Never before had I been treated so extravagantly like a queen. It was like a fairy tale come true. Then we packed everything in a Uhaul truck, and moved down to sunny, Sarasota, Florida.

We attended the church that Duane had been going to for nine years and I walked in the door feeling like it was just like my Grandparents' church I had grown up visiting all through my childhood. It felt like home. That church came to be family for us. My faith grew and so did my relationship with the Lord. We got involved in a Sunday school class where it was easier to get to know each other. There we talked about the Bible, how to learn a better way of life and grow closer to God. People were so genuine and caring there.

Change

I could see that God was changing me from within and making me a new person. Not that He's ever done changing us. He continues to work on me day by day.

Now, I have grown so much in wisdom, knowledge, peace, and joy *amidst* the struggles and trials. My life is like a fairy tale of hope and happiness that never has to end. Even on the days I doubt and lash out at the ones I love the most (I'm human), I have this firm hope that I will never give up. Jesus Christ has never let me down since that day I asked Him to take over my life.

I've grown and am so strong because of reading His word and my faith in Him. He has provided when I thought I might lose my life twice: I've had heart troubles and also hemorrhaged after I had given birth to my daughter, Daphne. During the beginning of my speaking ministry, we went through such lean years, I didn't know what I was going to feed my family that night, and God provided miracle after miracle to supply those meals and the rest of our needs. It wasn't always easy, but I've learned countless times over that, "The end blessings are always worth the struggle."

Chapter 5

We know that God works all things together for good for those that love Him and are called according to His purposes. Romans 8:28

I have a hope beyond anything that could take place on this earth that Jesus will make good of it all in the end whether I see it or not. I have learned this through reading the Bible and believing it's true. Getting involved closely with other Christians, asking questions, and studying the Bible and Christian books have helped me as well. Plants need the right amount of water, soil, and sunlight to flourish. In the same way, Christians need the Bible, church, and close Christian friends to flourish.

I urge you, if you don't know Jesus, ask Him into your heart right now. He has been calling to you all your life. He's the answer to questions that have no answers. He can fill the empty void that you have inside that you keep trying to fill with worldly things that never truly satisfy your heart, mind, and spirit. He is what you're searching for. He and His word can bring true contentment no matter what's going on around you. He will provide peace like no other. Love like no other. Joy like no other. He is the way, the truth, and the life. No one comes to God unless we invite Christ in first. John 3:16 says that God so loved the **world** (not just Christians) that whoever believes in Him will have everlasting life. Life beyond this world of pains. Life in heaven. So, I ask you, "What have you got to lose?" Write down some feelings or thoughts you have about this.

AMP Up Your Life

Chapter 5

Is there a reason you won't believe? Where you hurt by a Christian? There are good and bad Christians just like there are good and bad pastors, good and bad teachers, good and bad people. I wish this were a perfect world, but it's not. We're all imperfect, working and learning life at different places, being affected by different situations and upbringings. Take your eyes off the Christians and look at Jesus and His word.

Sometimes, it seems I have conquered Mt. Everest only to find another mountain of maturity I need to climb and master, to learn, grow, and gain wisdom. One thing I know is that pain causes me to cling to and run to my God. My question is, "What do *you* cling to when you *don't* have God?"

When I run to the Bible, God gives me hope, promises for a good future, for joy, and for heaven where there will be no more tears but dancing on golden streets. He tells me how to live life, when I do wrong, and how to correct myself and to stay positive. That's a huge reason I'm writing this book and why I go out and speak to women and share the gospel of Jesus Christ. How do people make sense of this life without God? I know what I've experienced, and it has been an amazing journey with Jesus Christ.

I have compassion for the pain I went through and the pains others must go through too. But I love my life and am so thankful God has changed me and blessed me with my blood family *and* my Christian family: A Christian family can span the whole earth: People you can connect with whom you've never met. We call them brothers and sisters in Christ.

Christians are people just like you, trying to be and do good and helping and supporting each other in that process.

Chapter 6
IF YOU REALLY WANT TO THRIVE

I heard Tony Robbins say once, "Thinking that we have no creator is like expecting a paper company to explode and out pops a dictionary."

Three thousand people got up on September 11, 2001, expected to see another day, but they didn't. They died when the twin towers fell to the ground. It could be the same for us. None of us know when our last day on this earth might be.

Don't wait until it's too late. Life is so short.

Do you want a guarantee *you'll* Thrive no matter what comes your way? He is the way, the truth and the life. Do you want to know Him today? Do you know Him but have lost touch with Him? Are you a Christian but have never fully committed yourself to Him to do anything He wants through you and to you?

I believe Jesus Christ died on a cross to save us from all our sins and then His Father God rose Him from the grave.

He is reaching out His hand to you right now. He can give you this free gift of life. You only need to ask Him into your heart and believe.

What have you got to lose?

You have nothing to lose and everything to gain! He is all powerful. He is infinite, without end, everlasting, omniscient, all-knowing, all-seeing, and without limit. Do you wonder what the purpose of life is? I believe it's to get to heaven and take as many people with us as possible.

Have you ever seen the Matrix series? I see God's spiritual world, as Neo sees *through* the computer generated world, to the real matrix. And just like Neo must believe, you must believe and decide which way you'll go; to belief or back to a simulation. The choice is always ours.

We once thought the earth was flat. Science tells us many things, but how do we know what's true? Like I said, you have nothing to lose in believing and everything to gain.

No matter what, we're on earth for a certain number of days to live out our lives. Look around and what do you see? I see a desk and computer. I see guitars and windows. All these things were created by a creator. How could you not think our earth and universe has a Creator? As I type I'm listening to a long playlist of film music and it's playing the music to the movie *Interstellar*. Is it a coincidence that I just talked about the universe? I think it's God winking at me?

Do you want to believe that you have an infinitely all-powerful God on your side?

Chapter 6

Hope is not the conviction that something will turn out well, but the certainty that something makes sense regardless of how it turns out.

My faith gives me ultimate hope in any situation. My faith gives me that "out"-look when I don't have any. Imagine life is a strong flowing river that we're swimming in. Now imagine stepping out of the river and just observing you living your life; your emotions, busyness, working, trials, crises. You're on the outside looking in. You can have a different outlook. You can separate yourself from life and see it for what it is. I believe I will spend eternity in heaven with Jesus. So even if my life were to end, I know where I will end up. The Bible tells me that God will right all things wrong, whether in this world or the next. He will judge everyone because He knows everything. He is totally in charge, but He gave us all free will to choose to do right or wrong here on earth. Romans 3:23 says, "All have sinned and fall short of the glory of God." Let's choose to do what's right. How do we know what's right and wrong anymore? The Bible has all the answers to what that *right* living is.

All you must do is *believe* in Him. *Believe* that God sent His Son, Jesus Christ, to die on the cross for your sins. I urge you to believe with all your heart. I implore you to love and trust Him with everything you have in you. **His** life is the fairytale when good always prevails in the end. It's the best movie ever when hope, determination, and great courage sees you through. And just like in the movies, there's evil that hurts us, but God has overcome the world! And He can help you overcome any worldly pain and suffering as well. He promises a perfect heaven where there will be no more tears or suffering. What have you got to lose in believing? My answer is absolutely nothing. Will life be perfect here on earth? No. It can't be because He gave us free will. But why not have a hope beyond any other hope that everything will work out in the end? He can help you overcome any problem. He can see you through any situation. *You* can do all things through *Him* who will give you strength.

For some of us, He changes us instantly, but for others, it takes time. What does it matter? The sooner you believe, the sooner you'll feel His amazing love permeate your life.

It's easy to pray to Him. Just speak to Him like you would a friend. "Dear Jesus, I want to believe you died for me. Help my unbelief. Give me faith. Come into my life and lead me and guide me. Forgive me for my sins. Save me from the pains of my past and present and future. Amen."

I sure hope you prayed that prayer. If you did, then welcome to the family of God. We're all brothers and sisters in Christ. It's so wonderful to have a family beyond your blood family. People you can trust and count on and ask for help. Are all Christians perfect? Absolutely not. Like I said, we're all in a process of learning to be more like Jesus. But I know one who *is* perfect, and that's Jesus Christ! *He* can give you the right perspective. He gives us the right outlook when we're struggling. He is the ultimate Savior to save you. Jump into His arms today. He will always be there for you waiting for you to ask Him in no matter what. No matter what you've

Chapter 6

done, or been through, He can wash you clean and make you whiter than snow.

Just like going without sweet treats and overindulgent foods, exercising and getting in great shape, taking one day at a time to get there, is always worth it because you feel so much better. One day at a time to feel better every day. He promises a future to prosper you and not harm you. We learn, grow, and gain more knowledge, wisdom, and His power.

How do you feel about Jesus? Do you believe? Do you doubt? Do you think you'll have to give up too much? He loves you just the way you are right now. Write out your thoughts.

_____

_____

_____

_____

_____

_____

_____

_____

_____

_____

AMP Up Your Life

Chapter 6

There are many people who have sat in church for years and never had a relationship with Jesus. Maybe they never made a commitment or total surrender to give up all rights and give Him permission to do anything he wants in them, to them, or through them? I believe that my prayer of surrender is what changed *me* from the inside out. It was painful at the time but it was the crucible that produced the change I longed for and needed.

All Up to Me

"Work like it all depends on you, and pray like it all depends on God."

Some days, I'm so caught up in myself and my work and that everything is up to me. I'm so full of myself, my wants, my needs, my here and now, and my feelings.

I have experienced so much pain. There comes a point when you have nothing left. No hope for tomorrow or no energy to fight for today, and you give up trying. But when you take God's hand and let Him lead the way, He can show you things you never thought possible. He can perform miracles and give you hope to go on.

> *Job 11:16-18 says, "You will surely forget your trouble, recalling it only as waters gone by. Life will be brighter than noonday, and darkness will become like morning. You will be secure, because there is hope; you will look about you and take your rest in safety."*

> *"Fear God and keep His commandments…for God will bring every deed into judgment, including every hidden thing whether it is good or evil."*
> *Ecclesiastics 12:13-14*

Are you living the life you want? Are you behaving at your best? Do you respect yourself? If you answered no, then do you think it might be time to make some changes? Sometimes we make excuses for ourselves and our actions. We think we just are the way we are, and that's a reason to *not* try to do anything different. It's a lie we tell ourselves. Or we believe we can't change. But we *can* change! Believe in yourself! Believe in God's power to help you as you pray to Him. Don't' ever stop trying and believing. Hope is what God always gives me. I can run to Him and His word and hope for the best. I can't always believe in myself because I'm far from perfect. We humans make mistakes, have accidents, and people hurt us. But God *is* perfect. He will never fail you. He says he sends His Holy Spirit to live *in* us and we are to walk in that Spirit instead of our own flesh. Sometimes, it's a battle to walk in His Spirit. We get caught up in the world and everything going on around us. I'm just thankful I have Him to run to, especially when I see my imperfection and failures. Remember, you can step out of the river to have a better outlook on your life passing by. Your whole life is there swimming in the current that never stops. But instead of being caught up in it, when you step out, you're observing it as a whole instead of just one moment.

Chapter 6

Does this analogy help you separate yourself from your emotions or trials? Life is short. Nothing lasts forever. This too shall pass. Write your feelings.

_____

_____

_____

_____

_____

_____

_____

_____

_____

_____

_____

_____

_____

_____

_____

AMP Up Your Life

Chapter 6

Jesus did not come to explain away suffering or remove it. He came to fill it with His presence.

For fifteen years, I thought life was just what I had gone through, of always suffering, always troubles, and always heartache. I lived many years *expecting* something to go wrong, someone to die, some way to be hurt. Pain and suffering was normal for me.

Can any of you relate? Ever feel like you're in a rotten life with no sign of escape? Do you feel like you're drowning, desperate for air, but no sign of the struggle ending? I've been there.

What do you want to see change about your life? What type of person do you want to be when you go through hard times?

_____

_____

_____

_____

_____

_____

_____

_____

Amp Up Your Life

Chapter 6

"I've Learned to Be Thankful"

Duane and I had two more children not quite two years apart when I was almost forty years old. I never thought I would get good sleep again. When they were maybe three and five I was still getting up with at least one of them every night, it seemed. In the middle of one night they both woke me up. I was so angry that I stomped up the stairs to try to settle them back down. I was seething inside about how difficult my days were with little sleep and how *I* usually have a hard time getting back to sleep. But in my anger, I remembered a Bible verse, "to give thanks in all things," so I just begrudgingly said to Him in my heart, "Lord, I give thanks for my children waking me up," even though I didn't feel it. Suddenly, I felt this peace enter my mind and heart. I got the children back to bed easily, and as I walked back down the carpeted stairs, I started singing a chorus to a song along with a verse. I wrote this down on a small pad of scratch paper in my nightstand drawer and as I was falling asleep, I knew I would wake up in the morning and finish the song, and I did. Now this has never happened before or since, to write a song in that manner. I believe it was God's gift to me for following His Word when it was hard. Here are the words to the song

> I don't know where I'm going, here or there
> Time it escapes my clutch my stare
> The revolving doors, oh their spinning fast
> But I fall at my Savior's feet at last

I've learned to be thankful for the rain
I've learned to be thankful for the pain
What the enemy tries to take away
I've learned to be thankful

Oh I'm on the edge and I'm spinning plates
Wonder when the next crash will seal my fate
The revolving doors oh their spinning fast
And I fall at my Savior's feet at last

This is the day that the Lord has made
Let us rejoice and be glad in it
Oh this is the day that the Lord has made
Let us rejoice and be glad in it

I've learned to be thankful

There are so many things out of our control. But, we *can* control our thoughts. God says to "give thanks in all things, and rejoice when you suffer trials of many kinds, because it produces perseverance." I know when you're in the middle of a storm, you can't begin to feel anything but despair, but I urge you to write or say the words, "Thank you God for this _____ (trial, difficulty)" even if you don't feel it.

In Phillipians4 it says, "Finally, brothers, whatever is true, whatever is noble, whatever is right, whatever is pure, whatever is lovely, whatever is admirable--if anything is excellent or praiseworthy--think about such things. Whatever you

CHAPTER 6

have learned or received or heard from me, or seen in me-- put it into practice.

Here He is telling us to think on good things, not the bad. It's easy to ruminate and swirl around the painful or sad thoughts. We can't change what has happened, but we can change how and what we think about these happenings. Choose to look for some small piece of good wherever you can.

> ***...the God of all comfort, who comforts us in all our troubles, so that we can comfort those in any trouble with the comfort we ourselves have received from God. For just as the sufferings of Christ overflow to us, so also through Christ our comfort overflows —2 Corinthians 1:4-5***

I can choose to believe I have gone through these painful trials so that I can be a comfort to others. I can empathize and sympathize with those who have gone through the same experiences, but I wouldn't be of much help if I didn't share and talk about it. I believe the truth will set you free. I believe our truths can help others.

God made laws to protect us, just like we have laws on earth to protect ourselves and others. It's always for protection.

Recap: Accept Jesus into your heart, start reading a Bible, get into church, and find or start a Bible study group

Chapter 7
WRITE YOUR STORY

Do you like to read? I love to read. Books are an amazing way to learn about everything. We learn everything by reading. And, if you don't like to read, you now have the capability to listen to audio books or watch videos on YouTube, as a way to learn. I have been reading non-fiction, self-help books all my life. I think these books have been my therapists so to speak. I have learned so much about life and learning and growing. People's words have inspired me and encouraged me in so many ways whether secular or Christian. And of course, the Bible is the best guide for life there is.

Writing down my biggest dreams and goals changed my life tremendously. Almost like magic. I didn't really expect them to happen. A couple things I accomplished from that dream list in the book, *Write It Down Make It Happen* that I wrote in 2015, was to quit my full-time job and to inspire and encourage women with my testimony, And I did quit my job and I now get to travel around the state of Florida speaking for a National Cristian Women's Organization sharing my testimony. This isn't something I set out to do, but God miraculously brought it into my life. But what I think is even more amazing is that just the other day when I went to grab the book to make sure I was spelling the authors name correctly, I started reading her instructions again about putting a star next to one that you think is grandiose or far-fetched. I looked at the page of goals I first wrote and the **one** with the star next to it that I thought could never happen was.....

to write a book!!

I couldn't believe what I was seeing. I have been frustrated because there are so many *other* things on my list that I haven't been able to accomplish so far, yet I'm doing one thing I never thought could be. I feel in my heart that God has led me where **He** wants me to go, not where ***I*** think I need to go. His timing is perfect even though we may not understand it, and His ways are perfect as well. He has proven this to me, over and over again. .

1 Corinthians in the Bible says to trust in the Lord with all your heart and lean not on your own understanding, but in all your ways acknowledge Him and He will make your path straight.

Trust in Him

Are you struggling with wanting certain things so badly, but you just can't seem to make yourself take the steps toward the goal? I would encourage you to trust in God's timing and keep taking the steps you *can* do. Every step will get you closer. Don't give up. I have been journaling almost daily ever since I read Henriette's book. The Bible talks about a time for war and a time for peace or a time to laugh and a time to cry. There are seasons in our lives that we must accept and trust in the process and timing and I believe we must do the same with what life gives us. Pray about it and trust in what you feel in your heart you need to work on. Trust in God and yourself.

And keep writing.

Goals

Dr. Gail Matthews, a psychology professor at the Dominican University in California, studied the art and science of goal setting. She gathered two hundred and sixty-seven people together, men and women from all over the world, and from all walks of life, including entrepreneurs, educators, healthcare professionals, artists, lawyers, and bankers. She divided the participants into groups, according to who wrote down their goals and dreams, and who didn't, She discovered that, "those who wrote down their goals and dreams on a regular basis were **42%** more likely to achieve them!" It's said that if you tell someone that you're going to do something, you have a 65% chance of achieving it, but if you have a person hold you accountable to a next step, then your probability of success jumps to **95%!**

Goals:

- Write them down.
- You must be very specific.
- They must be attainable.
- You must choose a time frame.
- Find an accountability partner.

Writing is worth the time

I think the time spent writing is totally worth it. I get out my frustrations, feelings, dreams, and all the possible ways to feel better and work out problems and ideas to accomplish those dreams or goals. By journaling, I answer a lot of my own questions when I look back and reread.

Do you hate the thought of writing? Do you think it's just a waste of time? That you're too busy? Journaling is like talking to a therapist but better. It's *free* and a huge time saver. You get an amazing emotional release by writing your feelings which reduces stress and anxiety. It helps you process your own thoughts and emotions and questions. I look back when I reread and realize that there are bad days, and that's all they are. Bad days come and go. And when another bad day comes, then I remember that my journaling reminded me that it will pass, and I can change my attitude even quicker.

Let it all out

My writers group talked about a brain dump. Just writing every thought and feeling and idea you have about something to get it all out. This is so creative because it can help you spark ideas you never would have thought of before.

In Julia Cameron's book, *The Artist's Way*, she said to write and fill three pages every morning as soon as you wake up. Write whatever pops in your head whether you're tired and weary-eyed or excited about starting your day. Maybe you can't think of anything to write. Just write out every feeling you have.

This is such a good practice as well, because so many of us deny our true feelings so much in our lives, especially in the presence of other people. "Hi, how is your day?" We might say "Fine" even though we really are frustrated. Writing exactly what pops in our brain allows us to practice accepting our *true* feelings.

We have so many dreams, desires, and goals, but most of the time, we squelch them all to go to work to make enough money to survive or to take care of our children, Life so easily gets in the way of what's most important, like being *happy* as a mom taking care of her children. Reading and writing helps me hone in on what's most important in life.

How many of us intend to lose weight, get more exercise, start a business, paint the house, eat healthier, or get more organized? The list goes on and on. Writing down those things helps trigger my subconscious to make them happen, like the act of putting on the work-out clothes and sneakers before I exercise. All those beforehand steps that need to be taken, must be implemented first. It's so easy for our brains to stop those steps before we even get started. We need to just do them or at least put them on the schedule.

The Most Important Thing

There's a lesson about taking a large glass vase and filling it with a set amount of sand, then a set amount of pebbles, then trying for a set amount of rocks. It won't all fit. But when you take the same set amount of rocks and put those in the vase first, *then* the pebbles, *then* the sand, it will all fit easily. It's the same in life as well as it is with our time. When we do the most important things first, all the small things will fit into place easily.

One example of this was at my lady's Bible study meeting. A mom had not come to our group for a very long time, and then finally came, and said how great it was to talk and visit and learn together. But at home before she left, she had looked at the dishes in the sink and wondered how on earth they would get done if she left. But they did get done of course, and she was so happy for taking the time to come and feel renewed and inspired. Do the right thing. Do the important thing. Trust that the small and urgent things *will* get done.

> *Gandhi said:"Happiness is when what you **think**, what you **say**, and what you **do** are in harmony."*

CHAPTER 7

Who are you?

Whenever there's a canyon between who you are and who you intend to be, it can cause depression, stress, and unhappiness. I lived a lot of years lying and deceiving myself in what kind of person I really was. I lived in de Nile. That river raft you hop on and just ride wherever it takes you. I had no thought to what kind of character I was portraying, what values were important, or what meaning my life had. These are important questions to ask yourself.

Another writing lesson I recently read by Dr. Peale is to write out **all** the negative things you're feeling and believe about yourself, and then start a fresh list of what you want your life to be like and who you aspire to be. He said to throw out the first list and then make copies of the second list and read it many times a day.

Sometimes, it takes half our life to learn who we really are and what we really like. You need to "find yourself," or to "feel good in your own skin." Many of us live so many years of our lives worried about what others think. We do everything based on what we *think* everyone else would do. God made *you* for a reason. He made your heart and mind. Trust Him, yourself, and your desires. He gave you those desires, as long as they are noble and good and don't go against what the Bible says.

Writing can improve other areas of your life

Small changes or habits that you might introduce into your routine might carry over into other aspects of your life.

Like momentum or leverage, you can feel the snowball effect and improve many areas just from one small change. For instance, when I was 45 pounds heavier, I decided I needed to lose weight and started exercising for 30 minutes every day. That's all I did. My body felt so much better exercising that I started eating less without thinking about it. I felt good about myself and was less stressed or depressed. I ended up losing the weight without a ton of work. Exercise was hard at first but became so much fun and effortless. Now, when I suffer from illness or injury, I realize how important exercise is to my mood when I haven't been able to do it. So, exercising, changing **one** thing had a profound effect on *multiple* things. Writing can do that for your life.

A few things I wrote were to be a certain weight, be energetic, and be *happy* to homeschool my children. This list is so helpful in reminding me of who I want to be, especially on the days when I don't feel good. It instantly peps me up and inspires me to be that person. Like momentum, the list propels my thoughts to have the positive uplifting attitude that I aspire to have.

Stick A Geranium In Your Hat And Be Happy

When I think of all the books that have meant so much to me, this one is at the top of the list. It was written by Barbara Johnson who endured somewhat similar experiences to me. Her husband was severely disabled in a car accident. She found out that one of her sons was gay and he left the family for 11 years. Another son died in Vietnam and another

Chapter 7

son was killed in a car accident exactly 5 years after the son in Vietnam. She admitted to thinking about committing suicide and sitting in her room staring at the wallpaper for a year.

I thought my family and my life was a mess, but reading her story told me that if she could be okay, then I could too. And that's why I'm writing. I want you to know that you can overcome any situation you're in, have gone through, or will go through.

Reading and writing has given me so much knowledge and help in life. I pray that they help you as well.

Chapter 8

"DO YOU HEAR WHAT I HEAR?"

How do we hear from God?
How do we have a relationship with Him?
How do we know if it's His voice or our own?
I'm no expert.

I only have my own path.
I only have what God has taught me so far. But I do see these as good questions to ask a pastor or other strong Christians and get their take on it. What has your experience been?
Many years ago, a friend of mine suggested we do a workbook together called, *Knowing and Doing the Will of God*, by Henry Blackaby and Claude King. This workbook helped me grow tremendously in *hearing* from God. They said that the Bible is God's word to you. Many times, we don't know which way to go or what choice to make.

Blackaby says, "God speaks to us by the Holy Spirit through the Bible, prayer, circumstances, and the church, to reveal Himself, His purposes, and His ways. What's God's will for *my* life, is not the right question.

The question should be…"

What's **God's** will?"

Matthew 6:34 says, But seek first His kingdom and His righteousness, and all these things will be given to you as well.

The focus needs to be on God, now our own lives.

I hear God's spirit speak to *me* through my natural instincts; through my gut. When I practice listening to the still small voice in small things, like being told to take the ponytail holder with me and not knowing why I would need it, and then needing it only a few minutes later, solidifies trusting that voice or instinct God gave me. I do this with the small things and then start to trust Him with slightly bigger things. It's so rewarding, as you do this more and more, and feel the trust building in your faith in Him. There's nothing more satisfying than trusting in yourself and that God *is* guiding you.

Hearing from God is a subject I want to study more. How do you feel about this subject? Take some time to journal. Do you think you hear from God? How do you know for sure?

Chapter 8

Chapter 9
BROKEN: WHEN YOU HAVE NO HOPE

Depression...

Are you there?

Are you empty?

I sit all day in a fog. I feel nothing but heartbreak and emptiness. Pain penetrates my soul deep inside my being. Nothing exists. There's no purpose or reason to do anything...

There's a dark, thick, ominous cloud enveloping me.

Can you relate?

Symptoms of a depressive episode can include:
- *Persistent* feelings of sadness or emptiness
- Feelings of hopelessness
- Loss of concentration and interest in hobbies
- Fatigue, lack of energy
- Thoughts of suicide and death

- Body aches
- Digestive problems
- Weight gain or loss

Causes - Clinical depression

- Stressful events. Most people take *time* to come to terms with stressful events, such as bereavement or a relationship breakdown
- Personality
- Family history
- Giving birth
- Loneliness
- Alcohol and drugs
- Illness
- Guilt from unresolved sin

It is difficult to share grief and sorrow when the proper Christian world is so in tune to joy and happiness. The depth of grief is seldom spoken of in the proper world and those in deep grief are afraid of being judged by those who cannot understand.

If we feel despair and hopelessness, than surely something is wrong with us. And we are judged as not being in proper communion with God? The deeply grieving hide their grief and sadness to avoid reprimand and rebuke.

In the scope of God's love, where is the concern and love for those stuck in the valley of death and grief, where the fruits of the spirit have fled from? Why are most people afraid

Chapter 9

of sickness and death when it is the only way to the glorious heaven we sing about?

–Delta Eash Partlo

I have been struggling with starting this chapter. Depression can be an intense season. I have been there, but it's been a long time. I want to let you know that it's okay if you're there, that you're not alone, and I believe that it's a *normal* response to particular events in our lives.

Here are excerpts of Mark Buchanan's article in intouch.org called

Embracing the Rhythms of Spiritual Growth:

I've lived through half a century of all four seasons, one after the next, though each different in its own way; winters so bleak I thought nothing could come out alive. I've been through muddy violent springs and blustery autumns. I've made a discovery that my heart has passed through many seasons too. I hardly noticed it.

What changed was a brutal winter of my soul. A close friend and a colleague died, and I didn't know where I was or what to do. I was sad and afraid, and very alone. I wanted to sleep during daytime. I stopped caring about things I cared about. I tried all manner of devices to snap myself out of it. I got more sleep, did more exercise, ate less sugar, and went on personal retreats. I underwent counseling, I considered medication. Nothing ended the duration of my winter.

But a slow awareness dawned: For everything there is a season. (Ecclesiastes 3:1) Unlike earth's seasons, our hearts seasons come in no particular order. Knowing this matters. Why? Because, in our prevailing ways of measuring spiritual maturity, we expect Christ followers to be perpetually fruit-bearing. Always up. Always on. We gauge spiritual maturity by how busy and upbeat we are. But is that what Jesus means when He says we are to bear much fruit, and by this glorify God?

I think not. Fruit implies seasons. Each season has its needed disciplines and distinct rhythms.

For everything there is a season. Take Jane. She and her husband Randy have always been "church people," sat on councils, headed youth and adult classes, taught Bible studies, and led worship. Then Randy confessed a pattern of repeated infidelities stretching back almost to the beginnings of their marriage. Jane tried to recover, but couldn't. Randy left. Jane is sitting in my office because she doesn't know who she is now and doesn't know what she believes. There are a few Jane's in all our churches, trying to figure out who they are, and where God is in their darkness and deep winter. Not many of them know that "for everything there is a season."

I'm a better pastor for Jane than I would have been a few years back. My own deep winter wasn't too long ago, and I can listen to her and wait with her in ways I couldn't before.

If your heart is in this season, there may be, hidden in its bleakness, a rare opportunity. You may be able to prune back unneeded responsibility, the burden of useless activity

Chapter 9

in exchange for simplicity. What can you cut and burn, and use the ashes to make the soil richer?

Each season has its own rhythms. As I've rethought my spiritual life from the perspective of seasons, I have given up a myth I long cherished; the quest for *balance*. I chased the golden mean for years, never catching it. I wanted to find the point of perfect equipoise between work and play and rest and family. But as I started to see my life and faith seasonally, I saw how little the idea makes sense. No season has anywhere near perfect balance. Each is lopsided one way or the next: too hot or too cold, too wet or too dry, too lush or too barren, too muddy or too parched. Seasons don't call for balance. They each require a pace and an option for moving through it that best matches that season's demands, its limits, and its opportunities.

For everything there is a season.

> *The **Beauty** of Brokenness*
> Broken people:
> Are overwhelmed with a sense of their own spiritual need
> Esteem all others better than self
> Surrender control
> Are humble
> Not concerned with self at all
> –Nancy Leigh DeMoss

Remember when I talked about Wabi Sabi, the Japanese art of beauty to be found in imperfection? Yesterday I tried doing everything I could to get in the mood to write this chapter, but to no avail. I even became physically ill and just gave up totally. So while I was journaling this morning and just feeling stuck with this chapter and not knowing where to start or what to say, I wrote, *"Embrace the Ughh."*

I knew I had to just dive into what it is. I'm not a counselor. I'm just sharing my feelings, experience, and observations in 53 years of living.

Depression sucks... Life sucks... Sometimes it's just pain... Cries of agony

I understand when you feel **no... strength**... Period!

I've been there. I'm sorry you're going through this depression for whatever reason it is, whether a loved one died, or someone broke up with you, you lost your job, or maybe you don't even know why for sure: you're just there.

You deserve to be happy again. You deserve a good life. Sometimes, it just takes *time*, the word no one wants to hear. Our world is so instant. We don't like waiting for much, do we?

Do you remember the story my mom wrote about being in my brother's messy room and crying out to God about her anger and hurt over his deadly disease?

Why don't you take time to write a letter to God about your depression and frustrations?

Be *totally* open and honest... He can handle the truth, for He says that the truth shall set you free.

Chapter 9

AMP Up Your Life

Chapter 9

AMP Up Your Life

Chapter 9

I left the last page blank in case you want to rip out the journal page and throw it away.

Chapter 9

When I'm in the Valley

When I'm on the mountain, the skies are filled with blue
When I'm on the mountain, then I don't praise you.
But when I'm in the valley, the skies area filled with gray.
When I'm in the valley, You teach me how to pray.
Then I cry, "Dear Jesus, You always see me through!"
When I'm in the valley, that's when I praise you.
When I'm on the mountain, the skies are filled with blue.
When I'm on the mountain, then I don't praise you.
When I'm in the valley, my eyes are filled with tears.
When I'm in the valley, I'm overcome by fears.
When I'm in the valley, that's when I praise you.
That's when I praise you. – John Marx

I've always talked to my children about the fact that, when we get sick and feel miserable, once we get better, we're so appreciative to have life back to *normal* again. It goes back to that word, perspective. When we aren't sick, we should be very grateful! But we soon forget. I think that's why the past is important to remember. Our past is how we learn things.

We will never know all the answers to life. When we're on the mountain (in the good times), we feel like we got there all by ourselves, but when we're in the valley (the bad times), we tend to ask God why.

I remember when the attack on the twin towers brought them exploding to the ground, and churches were filled with fearful, hurt people, crying out to God.

Don't Tell Me

There are no words to pray.
There are no words to say.
The spoken word is not enough,
to explain the pain of real tuff stuff
What to say and what to do.
When all the world is black and blue.
God is God and He is He.
All of this I plainly see.

*My brain is numb, my mouth can't speak.
I cannot see, I am so weak.
Don't tell me how to sleep at night,
Don't tell me how to pray.
Don't tell me how to live my life.
Don't give me words to say.*

*You haven't seen the world I've seen,
through blurry, tear filled eyes.
Or been to where I've been,
through pain and many lies.
Stand in the pouring rain
And feel the searing pain
Let it wash through you
Cool cleansing rain.*

*Don't tell me how to sleep at night
Don't tell me how to pray*

Don't tell me how to live my life
Don't give me words to say. –Delta Eash Partlo

Depression is not simply a medical problem or a mental problem, depression often is **a being human problem.**

"Why, if we are biologically coded for error, do we expend so much energy trying to appear as if we never make mistakes; that we know it all?"- Elizabeth Lesser

While medical and emotional problems can and often do contribute to depression, for others, this illness has very significant spiritual components.

You can find stories of the Bible where certain people experienced depression: Moses (Numbers 11: 10-16), David (Psalm 51; Psalm 32: 1-5), Elijah (1 Kings 19:1-18), Job, Jonah (Jonah 4:1-11), Psalmist (Psalm 73).

Larry Crabb, in his book Inside Out, emphasizes that our only hope for complete relief from hardship is to be with Jesus in heaven. "Until then," he says, "we either groan or pretend we don't. He adds, "The experience of groaning, however, is precisely what modern Christianity so often tries to help us escape."

Sometimes, we must groan...

And we need a hug, with no words...

As Christians, we may groan now, but there's glory ahead.

I consider that the sufferings of this present time are not worth comparing with the glory that is to be revealed to us. Romans 8:18

Do You Want Out of the Pit?

I'm thankful for my major depressive episode, because it brought the change that was necessary for my life. I learned from that experience that I **must** take care of myself both **physically** *and* **mentally**.

You may feel you have no power for anything, and you may not, and that's okay.

Oftentimes, you have foggy or clouded thinking. Just get through the day. Sometimes, that's the best you can do.

Getting professional medical help is always a good idea, especially if your depression is severe. In Ginger Zee's book *A Little Closer to Home; How I Found Calm After the Storm* (p. 245) she suggested, "For some folks, meditation and therapy aren't enough, and medication can be key just like a diabetic who has to take insulin daily."

There are many nonmedical solutions you can take to reduce your depression Just take one day at a time. Starting these self-help actions may seem challenging at first, but making a small change each day can quickly build momentum and increase your energy.

Suggestions for climbing out of the pit of depression:

Don't be afraid to ask for and get help. I have found that by just admitting there's a problem, and asking for help, starts a miraculous healing in itself. Accept the truth of where you

Chapter 9

are at and how you're feeling, but then bring your attention to these thoughts and activities that are helpful.

You can do this!

1. *Get some exercise.* Many scientific studies find that exercise is just as useful for relieving depression as medication, and has multiple health benefits. I suggest a walk outside every day for ten or twenty minutes, and work your way up to thirty walking as fast as you can.
2. *Challenge your negative thought patterns.* Thoughts such as, "I have no hope," "I'm empty and have nothing left to give," or "I will be stuck here forever," are common in a depressed person's mind. Those negative thoughts become an unconscious habit, reinforcing the feeling of depression. Challenge those negative thoughts. Remember the times when you *did* feel differently about life, when you had hope and desires, or energy and motivation. Believe you'll get it back. **Believe** you can climb your way out of the pit.
3. *Eat healthy foods.* Junk food brings temporary comfort, but ultimately it's hazardous to your health and only adds to a deeper depression. Concentrate on wholesome foods only, like lean meats, and fresh vegetables, and fruits.
4. *Try to get good sleep.* For example:
    - Go to bed at the same time every night

- Don't eat for at least two to three hours before bed.
- Don't drink caffeine before bed and try to slowly cut down your caffeine intake throughout the day
- Listen to positive, calming motivational messages or sermons.
- Read the Bible or a nonsuspenseful book in bed.

5. *Drink plenty of water* throughout your day.
6. *Make a change in routine.* You can often get in a routine that reinforces the symptoms of depression. If you find yourself doing the exact same things every day and feeling depressed, try something different, like more of the suggestions in this list.
7. *Get a routine.* Maybe you need more structure by establishing a routine. For example getting up and **getting dressed** in the morning or going for that **walk.** Call a friend or write in a **journal** about things you *can* be thankful for.
8. *Try to laugh.* Watch funny movies, read jokes, or listen to comedians on you tube.
9. *Help someone else.* Call a friend and ask if they need help with anything, volunteer at a local charity or thrift store, help a neighbor with yard work, or adopt a pet.
10. *Getting out your emotions*, can be very helpful. Write in a journal, call a friend, look for and join a

Chapter 9

support group or, if you can't find one, start one at a local church or library.

Beware of spending too much time looking back at what you once were, when God wants you to become something you have never been. –Oswald Chambers

Another idea that might be helpful is to have a cry session. Set a timer for thirty minutes to cry and feel all the sadness you can, then when the time is up, get up and go do something physical. The next day do the same, but set the timer for one minute less, and so on and so on, daily until you have no minutes left.

Years ago when I was in that deep state of depression, a Sunday school teacher taught, "If you feel isolated and down, it's because of captivity not obedience." Repeating that saying, has helped me a lot over the years. It says to me, that Satan wants me captive in feeling *isolated* and *depressed*, and if I stay feeling that way, I'm giving into his wishes. I surely don't want to give into Satan. But we should be obedient to God's word that tells us to be thankful in all things (1 Thessalonians 5:18), to rejoice in the Lord always (Phillipians 4:4), and to trust that God works all things together for good for those that love Him (Romans 8:28).

Follow me one step at a time. That is all I require of you. You see huge mountains looming ahead, but the path may take an abrupt turn, leading you toward an easy path. Keep your mind on the present journey, enjoying my Presence. Walk by faith, not by sight (2 Corinthians 5:7), trusting Me to open up the way before you.

Chapter 10
YOU GOT THIS

I've written a lot of dreams and goals. Jack Canfield says to write 101 goals, but Brooke Castillo instructed me to write only the *five* most important goals for my life. I really had to stop and think for several days about what was most important. When I wrote them, they were a mix of goals, virtues, and values to live by. Please take time now to stop and think about the five most important things you should focus your life on right now for this season you're in. You may even change a few things later. I did.

Remember life is short. You could die tomorrow or next year. What do you want your life to mean on this earth? God created you for a special reason. No other person on the planet has what *you* have to offer. God made us in his image to think, love, laugh, imagine, create, plan, and speak, but most importantly, the power to choose. What do you really want? What do you really enjoy doing that makes your heart soar? What's the right thing to do because you know it's the right thing to do?

Write your five most important goals:

1. _____
2. _____
3. _____
4. _____
5. _____

Don't be afraid to be you.

The world needs your thoughts, feelings, and interpretations. I recently read a book by Marie Forleo called, *Everything Is Figureoutable*. She says, "When you have an idea, the tiniest dream for yourself or others, and you **don't** do everything you can to bring it to life…then you're stealing from those who need you the most." We're withholding from others what can help them.

Now my analytical brain thinks about all the people that dream of doing bad things like murder and rape, etc. I definitely don't want to encourage anything of that nature; do you? So I would add, "as long as it doesn't go against the *law* or against the word of God. And in addition, nothing we do, should *hurt* another person or encourage them to do anything wrong.

Fear

When I was working on my first speech, and planned to travel around the state and share my story with ladies groups, I knew I needed to ask my dad's permission about sharing the truth of his homosexuality in public. I was completely terrified of asking him. We had hardly talked about his lifestyle over the years, and I had this deep pit of nervousness in my stomach, but I mustered up the courage and asked. I explained, "Dad, I really want to share this because I want to let people know they're not alone." He responded, "Okay." I fought through that angst, and was relieved and surprised at how easy the conversation went. But why was it so hard and why was I fearful?

Why do we have fear about things?

Jack Canfield says that FEAR stands for:

F-alse

E-vidence

A-ppearing

R-eal

The first time I called a restaurant to ask if we could go play music, I was nervous and unsure. But once I did it, I realized it was no big deal. Sometimes, those *first-time* situations trip us up, like when we start a new job and are unsure about procedure specifics.

The five core fears are:
1. Failure
2. Success
3. Disapproval/Rejection
4. Losing Control/ Uncertainty
5. Death

Experts say that 90% of the things we worry about never happen. As far as success goes, "Who are you *not* to become great?" So many times, we only deal with absolutes in our minds. We only do or say things that we're 100% sure of accomplishing. But Sam Dogen says that we should think in probability. If there's a 70% chance of succeeding, then we should go for it.

Life is too short to worry or fear!

The Bible says 365 times, not to worry!

For years, starting at the time my daughter was only two years old, she would develop asthma whenever she got sick with a cold. There were many occasions when she would cough so much, she couldn't catch her breath and I would begin to have this fear and anxiety that would grip me in the pit of my stomach and would last as long as her illness would. I would sleep on my little four-year-old daughter's floor, in vigilance to monitor her cough and need of breathing treatments. I was extremely tense and would jump and stir at every noise and cough, so sleep was patchy.

After years of this happening, and having to take her to ER many times, two occasions with 103.5 temperature along with the asthma, I got so anxious about it that I thought I would die from the stress and anxiety. One night in the middle of what felt like a continuous panic attack, I had to ask myself,

"What's the worst thing that could happen?"

With much trepidation, I answered,

Chapter 10

"She could die."

"And I would be devastated and heartbroken, but she would be in heaven in pure bliss."

Speaking out that possibility helped me face my fear and anxiety head on. It was the truth. It was life as it is. *Not only did it release most of my panic, but helped me think about what I could control and do for her now. Staying in that continual state of panic was only eating me alive.*

What's your biggest fear that you must overcome? Is there any truth to it? What are the probabilities? Should you curl up into a ball and hide away because of it? Or do you want to face it head on and step over it with ease?

_____

_____

_____

_____

_____

_____

_____

AMP Up Your Life

_____

_____

_____

_____

_____

_____

_____

And the time came when the risk to remain in a bud was more painful than the risk it took to blossom. _ Elizabeth Lesser

You picked up this book to blossom. You're ready to peel away the layers and break through the cocoon to become the butterfly. Jesus says to let your light shine from the mountain top.

You are the light of the world. A city on a hill cannot be hidden. Neither do people light a lamp and put it under a basket. Instead, they set it on a stand, and it gives light to everyone in the house. Matthew 5:14

Chapter 10

Feel like you're gonna drown?
Step out of the current that was pulling you down.
Let Him part the sea of your heartache.
Never again will you break
For His strength you shall take.

For you are now strong, and you belong.
The world needs your offering
To make their souls sing.

You are ready to Thrive!
It's time to come alive.
Spread your wings and take flight.
The moment has arrived. -Deanne Kauffman

Don't let fear stop you from accomplishing what you're really supposed to be doing with your life.

I've heard people say, "The thing you fear the most, is what you should do." And this has been true for my life. I encourage you to fight your fears and just do the *thing*. (As long as it isn't against the law, or the word of God, or hurts anyone)

Even if you *don't* get a yes, or accomplish your goal, you can be proud of overcoming the fear and ***trying***! One step forward is one step forward. Doing nothing gets you nowhere.

You Can Thrive!

AMP UP YOUR LIFE

The Name of Jesus

Again, I implore you to be a follower of Jesus Christ. You have nothing to lose and everything to gain. He can give you the strength to face life with **no fear**. Not even *death*. I believe when I die, I will go to heaven where there will be no more trials or pain, but only Jesus' bright light shining on my face that will never have to shed another tear.

He can fill any empty void this world cannot. His **word** and promises can bring you a much greater "high" than any drug or accomplishment ever could.

Have you ever wished that you had a book to tell you what's right or wrong, or how to live this life? You do! It's the Bible. These are the Ten Commandments:

1. No other gods, only Me.
2. Do not bow down or serve any image.
3. No using the name of God in curses or silly banter.
4. Remember the Sabbath day and rest.
5. Honor your father and mother.
6. Do not kill.
7. Do not commit adultery.
8. Do not steal.
9. Do not lie.
10. Do not covet what another has.

I would suggest starting out with reading the New Testament first. Another place to start with or combine with reading the New Testament is reading Psalms and Proverbs. There's so much common sense and wisdom in the Bible.

CHAPTER 10

> *The greatest thing I have gained and learned from following Jesus is the ability to have contentment no matter what the circumstance! -Deanne Kauffman*

Wouldn't you like to be able to say that; to feel that? Nothing and no one in this life is perfect. Not even computers! Aren't they supposed to be perfect? You would think they would be being programmed and all.

I quite often say to people when a computer system isn't working like we want it to, "Computers are just like people, they don't always do what they're supposed to do."

But JESUS is perfect!

And *you* could have this perfect God backing you up. He will teach you and show you the way. God loves you no matter who you are, what you've done, or how far you **run**. He will *always* have His arms open wide for you just as you are.

No matter how dirty you feel.
No matter how unworthy you feel.
No matter how lost you feel.

It is never too late!

This is my story…
What's yours?

Too many people are thinking of security instead of opportunity. They seem to be more afraid of life than death. The purpose of life is a life of purpose.
—Robert Byrne

What's your purpose on this earth? You have greatness in you ready to burst forth from the ashes of whatever you've gone through. Now is your time to break free and fly.

Is it easy to stay a caterpillar? Yes.
Can we be happy staying a caterpillar? Yes.
But, we were born to become **butterflies**.

Remember wabi sabi. Embrace the struggle and changes.

There are only two ways to live your life. One is as though nothing is a miracle. The other is as though everything is a miracle. —Albert Einstein

You Are a Miracle to the World!

Chapter 10

<u>*You've got what it takes so*</u>
<u>*Go*</u>
<u>*To it!*</u>
<u>*Show them what you're made of. (the love)*</u>
2 Corinthians 8:10-24 The Message Bible.

Wrap-Up

I want you to go back through the book and reread your notes. What did you tell yourself you must do? What gave you hope? What actions will you take today, this week, this month? Now prioritize what's **the** most important? Put it on your calendar or to do list, and do it *first*, before everything else. Remember, the big rocks must go in the jar first.

What Do You Want?

Life is too short to not do the things you want. Now is the time. What do you plan to do with your one wild and precious life? **Believe** that you **deserve** what you desire and **believe** that **God** gave you those **desires.**

> *"You'll never regret spending your life doing things that make you happy." –Mel Robbins*

List all the actions you need to take:

_____

_____

AMP Up Your Life

Chapter 10

_____

_____

_____

_____

_____

_____

_____

_____

_____

_____

_____

Now list the words that set you on fire and gave you the most hope:

_____

AMP Up Your Life

Chapter 10

_____

_____

_____

_____

Amp up your thoughts.

Take control of the messages going on in your head. Your attitude, mindset, and perspective make all the difference.

1. What's your attitude about life, your relationships, your work, and the current issues you're facing today? What *truths* do you need to replace the lies that are on replay in your mind?
2. Have you lived all your life with a mindset about certain things that needs to be changed with something much more productive? The mindset we hold about things, situations, and circumstances has a great effect on our reality. What's a negative mindset you've had that needs to be changed to a positive one?
3. Have you learned that you can change your perspective about certain situations in your life? What are they?

_____

_____

Chapter 10

_____
_____
_____
_____
_____
_____
_____
_____
_____
_____
_____

Enjoy Life

Are you enjoying your days? What can you do to make your day more fun? An outing with a friend? A vacation? Try

Chapter 10

to come up with more ideas than you did in that chapter. Fun, fun, fun. What makes you laugh?

Write Your Story

Do you feel more open to sharing your story? We're only as sick as our secrets. When we share our truths, it lets others know that we're all human and we all have good times and bad. This is very important in this age of online social media where we only see small pieces of life that are usually only good things. Did you buy a journal? I really think you should. Write your heart away and discover how to Thrive through your writing. Keep writing how you *want* to feel.

The Send Off

Take care of your body and learn more about healthy nutrition and exercise and implement what you learn. Your health is more important than anything else. It's the foundation to a good life.

For all the moms and dads out there struggling with raising your children, my thoughts and prayers are with you as you raise the next generation. It's the *most important* job in the world. A very good friend of mine wrote this poem:

SOME DAYS
In the land full of children
Where I lived for so long,
There was so much to do,
Life moved quickly along.
Some days filled with laughter

Amp Up Your Life

But too many were just full,
For there were errands and chores,
And work and school.

Still some days filled with playgrounds
And slides and swinging,
And others with giggles and reading
And singing.
Some days filled with waves and
Water and sand,
Some of the days in this children filled land.

But it's for certain they were far,
Far too few,
For there were much too many
things to do.
I turned away for a moment;
It wasn't long,
And when I looked back, the
Children were gone.
Through the land of lost children
I searched everywhere;
I looked and looked but
They were not there.

Finally to the land of grown children I came.
It was there that I found them
But they were not the same.

Chapter 10

*So if you find yourself
In this child-land today,
Don't be quick to leave
And don't turn away;
Not for one single moment
Or this lesson you will learn.
Once you leave this land
You can never return.* –Susan Blount, The Hand of The Most High

Jesus

In my experience, it wasn't until I gave up all myself to the will of God and asked Jesus to take complete control over me; to lead me and guide me and to do anything He wanted to me or through me, that I was transformed into a new person and the began the journey of letting go of my painful past.

There's nothing more fun and more exciting than knowing Jesus and doing His will. Following His call will be the most rewarding, challenging, growing, and learning experience you could ever have. The greatest thrill ride imaginable. Better than any drug-induced high or drunken weekend. We don't need to run to food or run to escape anything when we can run to Him. He will supply all your needs. Let Him show you.

You can have His **peace** no matter what.

But *you must* take the step to invite Him in. If you have made this decision for the first time, to accept Jesus, please contact me at <u>deannekauffman4@gmail.com</u>. I would love to hear about it. Now go find a church, get into a Bible study group and start a new life. Tell everyone that you just made this decision. Remember, the truth will set you free. And set others free as well.

Trials will always come. This is a part of life.

> But you're an Overcomer
> Stay in the fight till the final round
> You're not going under
> Cause God is holding you right now
> You might be down for a moment
> Feeling like it's hopeless
> That's when He reminds you
> You're an Overcomer -Mandisa

Taken from Our Daily Bread 2004

I was at ease, but He has shattered me. —Job 16:12

Ground Squirrels hibernate near our home during the winter, and they appear when the snow melts in the spring. My wife Carolyn and I enjoy watching them scurry back and forth from one hole to another, while others stand like tiny sentries watching for predators.

In mid-May, a man from a nearby golf course arrives on a little green tractor with a tank loaded with lethal gas. The

Chapter 10

groundskeeper tells us that these little critters have to be eliminated because they dig holes in the fairways. Some survive, but most do not. It always makes us a little sad to see the tractor arrive.

If I could, I'd chase the little animals away. I'd destroy their holes and force them to settle someplace else. I'm sure they would resent my interference, but my actions would be solely for their good.

So it is with God. He may break up our comfortable nests now and then, but behind every difficult change lies His love and eternal purpose. He is not cruel or capricious; He is working for our ultimate good (Romans 8:28). He wants us to be "conformed to the image of His Son" (v.29) and to give us glorious enjoyment in heaven forever. How then can we fear change when it comes from Someone whose love for us never changes? (vv38-39). David Roper

God's love can seem harsh until we view it with hindsight

Trust in Him and His purpose and ultimate plan

We all go through a continuing education of life. Embrace it. Enjoy it.

Now get out there and Dream Big! AMP Up Your Life! Have faith in yourself!
Believe you have what it takes to not only survive, but Thrive! And Never Ever Give Up!

AMP UP YOUR LIFE

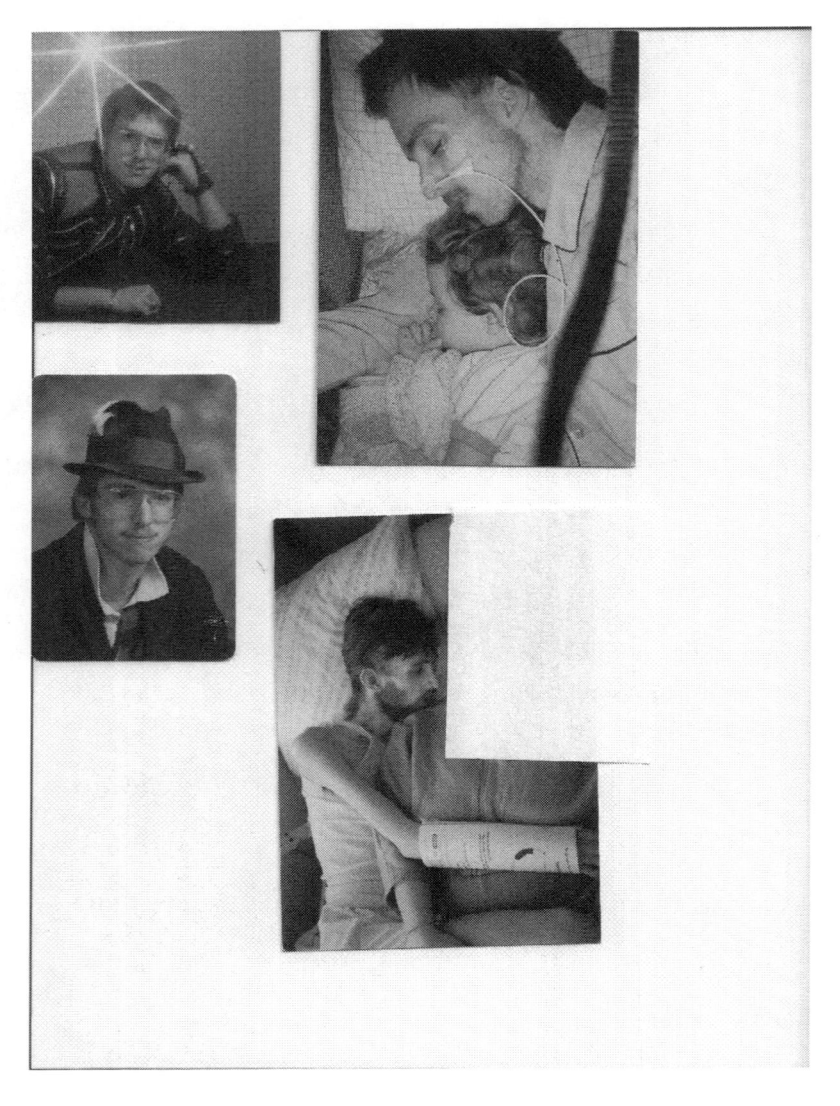

Figure 1 Dale's graduation pictures and then in a hospital bed in our living room.

Chapter 10

Figure 2 The gathering for quilts made for all those that lost their life to AIDS.

My daughter's rendition of my brother's graduation picture.

Suggested Reading/ Citations:

Blackaby, Henry T. King, Claude V. *Experiencing God: Knowing and Doing the Will of God.* Nashville, TN. Lifeway Press, 1990.

Buchanon, Mark. *Embracing the Rhythms of Spiritual Growth.* Intouch.org. Used with permission.

Blunt, Susan. *The Hand of the Most High: Inspirational Scripture & Verse.* Sarasota, Florida. Peppertree Press, 2008

Cameron, Julia. *The Artist's Way: A Spiritual Path to Higher Creativity.* New York, New York. Putnam, 1992.

Canfield, Jack. *The Success Principles: How to Get from Where You Are to Where You Want to Be.* New York, New York. Harper Collins Publishers, 2005.

TEDx. October 15, 2014. Traverse City *Dr Alia Crum, Change Your Mindset, Change The Game. TEDx* (VIDEO) https://youtu.be/npr5bg20_78

David Rober, *Our Daily Bread®* Copywrite© 2004 by Our Daily Bread Ministries, Grand Rapids, MI. Reprinted by permission. All rights reserved.

DeGraaf, Tracy. *Laugh Anyway, Mom: Hilarious Survival Stories from a Mother of Five Who Has Learned How to Keep the Joy in Motherhood (and How YOU Can Too)!)*! 2010.

Ditchfield, Christin. *What Women Should Know About Letting It Go: Breaking Free from the Power of Guilt, Discouragement, and Defeat.* Abilene, Texas. Leafwood Publishers, 2015.

Erwin, John and Andrew, 2014. Youtube (*Mom's Night Out scene: God's Love for Moms*). YouTube, 2014.

Ford, Debbie. *Courage: Overcoming Fear and Igniting Self-Confidence.* New York, New York. Harper One, 2012.

Frankl, Victor E. *Man's Search For Meaning.* Boston, Massachusetts. Beacon Press, 1959.

Johnson, Barbara. *Pain Is Inevitable but Misery Is Optional so, Stick a Geranium in Your Hat and Be Happy.* Dallas, London, Vancouver, Melbourn. Word Publishing, 1990.

Klauser, Henriette Anne. *Write It Down, Make It Happen: Knowing What You Want and Getting It.* New York, New York. Touchstone, 2000.

Marx, Fran. *When I'm In The Valley, by John Marx.* your-successadvocate.com

Meyer, Joyce. *Battlefield of the Mind: Winning the Battle in Your Mind.* New York, New York. Warner Books, 1995.

Stanley, Charles. *How to Handle Adversity*. Nashville, Tennessee. Thomas Nelson, 1989.

Ten Boom, Corrie. *The Hiding Place*. Minneapolis, Minnesota; World Wide Publications, 1971.

Tracy, Brian. *Maximum Achievement: Strategies and Skills That Will Unlock Your Hidden Powers to Succeed.* New York, New York. Simon & Schuster, 1993.

Whelchel, Lisa. *Taking Care of the Me in Mommy: Becoming a Better Mom- Spirit, Body & Soul.* Nashville, Tennessee. Thomas Nelson, 2006.